OTHER TITLES OF INTEREST FROM GR/ST. LUCIE PRESS

Medicolegal Issues for Radiographers, 3rd Edition

Total Quality in Radiology: A Guide to Implementation

Textbook of Total Quality in Healthcare

Pain Management

Home Health Care: Principles and Practices

Quality Care: Prescription for Injecting Quality into Healthcare Systems

Healthcare Book of Lists

Healthcare Hazard Control and Safety Management

Healthcare Teams: Building Continuous Quality Improvement

The Handbook of Management and Organizational Behavior in Healthcare

Florida Healthcare and Legal Guide

Principles and Practices of Disability Management in Industry

Principles of Fluoroscopic Image Intensification and Television Systems

Workbook and Laboratory Manual

Principles of Fluoroscopic Image Intensification and Television Systems

Workbook and Laboratory Manual

Robert J. Parelli, M.A., RT(R)

CRC Press is an imprint of the
Taylor & Francis Group, an **informa** business

First published 1997 by GR/St. Lucie Press

Published 2018 by CRC Press
Taylor & Francis Group
6000 Broken Sound Parkway NW, Suite 300
Boca Raton, FL 33487-2742

First issued in hardback 2018

© 1997 by Taylor & Francis Group, LLC
CRC Press is an imprint of Taylor & Francis Group, an Informa
business

No claim to original U.S. Government works

ISBN 13: 978-1-138-46489-6 (hbk)
ISBN 13: 978-1-57444-082-9 (pbk)

This book contains information obtained from authentic and highly
regarded sources. Reasonable efforts have been made to publish
reliable data and information, but the author and publisher cannot
assume responsibility for the validity of all materials or the
consequences of their use. The authors and publishers have attempted
to trace the copyright holders of all material reproduced in this
publication and apologize to copyright holders if permission to publish
in this form has not been obtained. If any copyright material has not
been acknowledged please write and let us know so we may rectify in
any future reprint.

Except as permitted under U.S. Copyright Law, no part of this book
may be reprinted, reproduced, transmitted, or utilized in any form by
any electronic, mechanical, or other means, now known or hereafter
invented, including photocopying, microfilming, and recording, or in
any information storage or retrieval system, without written
permission from the publishers.

For permission to photocopy or use material electronically from this
work, please access www. copyright.com (http://www.copyright.com/)
or contact the Copyright Clearance Center, Inc. (CCC), 222 Rosewood
Drive, Danvers, MA 01923, 978-750-8400. CCC is a not-for-profit
organization that provides licenses and registration for a variety of
users. For organizations that have been granted a photocopy license by
the CCC, a separate system of payment has been arranged.

Trademark Notice: Product or corporate names may be trademarks
or registered trademarks, and are used only for identification and
explanation without intent to infringe.

Visit the Taylor & Francis Web site at
http://www.taylorandfrancis.com

and the CRC Press Web site at
http://www.crcpress.com

The copyright owner's consent does not extend to copying for general
distribution, for promotion, for creating new works, or for resale. Specific
permission must be obtained from GR/St. Lucie Press for such copying.

This book is dedicated to my mother,
Antionette Parelli,
with love.

In memory of my father,
Charles J. Parelli, Sr.,
who loved and inspired
both of his sons.

Contents

Preface xiii

Author xv

Chapter 1: Image Intensifier System 1

Image Intensifier Tube Design 2

Input Phosphor and Photocathode 2

Electrostatic Focusing Lens 4

Accelerating Anode 4

Output Phosphor 5

Dual Field Image Intensifier Tubes 5

Conversion Factor and Gain 7

Flux Gain 8

Minification Gain 9

Image Quality 10

Automatic Brightness Stabilization 13

Review Questions 18

Chapter 2: Objective and Camera Lenses 21

Optics 21

Real and Virtual Images 25

Review Questions 27

Chapter 3: Closed Circuit Television Systems 29

Camera Pick-Up Tubes 30

Video Signal 33

Television Scanning System 35

Camera Control Unit 37

Synchronization 38

Television Monitor 39

Television Image Quality 41

Plumbicon and Image-Orthicon Cameras 43

Review Questions 45

Chapter 4: Recording the Television Image 47

Magnetic Recorders 48

Video Tape Recorders 51

Cinefluororadiography 53

Spot-Film Camera System 57

© GR/St. Lucie Press

■ Principles of Fluoroscopic Image Intensification and Television Systems: Workbook and Laboratory Manual

Film/Screen Spot-Film Device 58
Equipment Requirements 60
Review Questions 63

Chapter 5: Computerized Fluoroscopic Image Intensification 65
Computerized Fluoroscopy 65
Mask Mode Image Intensification 66
Time Interval Difference (TID) Mode.......................... 67
K-Edge Image Intensification 68
Combination vs. Unmixed Digital Techniques 68
X-ray Exposure with Computerized Image
Intensification 69
The Future of Computerized Image Intensification 70
Review Questions 72

Chapter 6: Fluoroscopic Image Production 73
Electromagnetic Radiation 73
Production of X-radiation 76
X-ray Interaction with Matter 79
Review Questions 83

Chapter 7: Factors Affecting Patient and Operator Exposure 85
Review Questions 91

Chapter 8: Health Effects of Low Level X-ray Exposure 93
Somatic Dose Indicators 93
Genetic Dose Indicators 94
Genetically Significant Dose 95
Review Questions 96

Chapter 9: Biological Effects and Significance of X-ray Exposure ...97
Cellular Amplification 97
Gross Cellular Effects of Radiation 98
Latent Period 98
Dose Effect Curves 99
Radiosensitivity of the Cell 100
Short-Term Effects.. 101
Long-Term Effects 101
Review Questions 104

Chapter 10: Personnel Radiation Protection 105
ALARA.. 105
Operator Protection during Image Intensification
Procedures 106
Other Protective Devices and Accessories 110
Review Questions 111

© GR/St. Lucie Press

■ Contents

Chapter 11: Personnel Monitoring 113
    Film Badge 115
    Thermoluminescent Dosimeter (TLD) 115
    Pocket Ionization Chambers 116
    Maximum Permissible Dose (MPD) 116
    Occupational and General Dose Equivalent Limits.... 117
    Frequency of Exposure Recording 117
    Overexposure of a Personnel Monitoring Device 118
    Cumulative Occupational Dose Equivalent 118
    Location of Personnel Monitoring Device 118
    Who Must Be Monitored 119
    Review Questions 120

Chapter 12: Pediatric Fluoroscopy 121
    Motion 122
    Personnel and Parental Protection 123
    Gonadal Shielding 123
    Automatic Exposure Control (AEC) 123
    Other Technical Considerations 124
    Review Questions 125

Chapter 13: Mobile Image Intensification Equipment 127
    Structural Provisions 127
    Equipment Provisions (Mobile C-Arm) 128
    Boost Position (High-Level Control Button) 129
    Mobile Fluoroscope Quality Control 129
    Review Questions 130

Chapter 14: California Radiation Control Regulations—
Responsibility of the Supervisor and Operator 131
    Restrictions 133
    Display of Documents 134
    Record Keeping Requirements 135
    Incident Notification Requirements 135
    Required Training and Information Provided to
        X-ray Users 136
    X-ray Equipment Safety Provisions 137
    Supervision of Radiologic Technology Personnel 137
    Technologists' Fluoroscopy Clinical Instruction 139
    Reduction in Dose 140
    Scheduling Radiologic Examinations for Women of
        Child-Bearing Years 142
    Therapeutic Abortions 143
    Occupationally Exposed Women of Procreative Age 144

Principles of Fluoroscopic Image Intensification and Television Systems: Workbook and Laboratory Manual

Summary of Gonad Shielding in Diagnostic
Radiology 146
Visual Physiology 148
Half Value Layer (HVL) 150
Review Questions 151

Chapter 15: Three-Dimensional Fluorographic Anatomy 153
Fluoroscopic Localization Techniques 153
Gallbladder Fluoroscopy 155
Terminal Ileum Fluoroscopy 155
Knee Arthrography 156
Review Questions 158

**Chapter 16: Fluoroscopy Quality Assurance and Quality Control
Program 159**
Principles of a Quality Assurance Program 160
Quality Assurance Program for Fluoroscopic
Systems and Associated Equipment 161
Acceptance Testing 166
Establishment of ALARA 168
Fluoroscopy Equipment Quality Control Tests and
Frequency 168
Review Questions 176

Appendix A: Answers to Review Questions 177

Appendix B: Statement of Competency 181

Appendix C: Review Test/Answers 183

Appendix D: Laboratory Experiments 195
Lab #1: Scatter Radiation 197
Lab #2: Source-to-Table-Top Distance 201
Lab #3: Grid Alignment... 205
Lab #4: Fluoroscopic Resolution Test 209
Lab #5: Maximum Fluoroscopic Exposure Rate 211
Lab #6: Fluoroscopy Low Contrast Performance 215
Lab #7: Automatic Exposure Control Evaluation
for Film Recording System/Reproducibility 217

Appendix E: Glossary 221

Appendix F: Bibliography 231

Index... 233

© GR/St. Lucie Press

Preface

Principles of Fluoroscopic Image Intensification and Television Systems: Workbook and Laboratory Manual introduces to the reader the subjects of fluoroscopic equipment, image intensification, closed circuit television systems, image recording devices, and three-dimensional anatomy, including information regarding quality assurance for fluoroscopic equipment. The emphasis throughout this workbook is on the practical application of the theory and principles of fluoroscopic image intensification to include radiation protection and radiation monitoring devices that are listed in Chapters 10 and 11.

Pediatric fluoroscopy and mobile image intensification are discussed in Chapters 12 and 13. More specifically, Chapter 14 covers Radiation Control Regulations which are specific to California State Laws relating to Fluoroscopic Certification.

The purpose of *Principles of Image Intensification and Television Systems: Workbook and Laboratory Manual* is to review the theories and principles of fluoroscopic image intensification and to investigate them in a logical and practical manner. Throughout this workbook, the reader will discover and examine those principles of image intensification and television systems that contribute to the sharpness and visibility of the image.

More importantly, the laboratory exercises were prepared as quality control procedures that can be used as part of the quality assurance program for any diagnostic imaging department.

All the chapters have learning objectives and chapter review questions. A detailed 100-question test has been designed to assist the reader in preparing for both State Licensure and National Registry Certification. Answers to the chapter review questions and review test are found on pages 177–180 and 194.

The reader should feel comfortable in learning and retaining the concepts listed in the workbook. I firmly believe that the knowledge gained from this workbook will expand the knowledge base and research base of the radiography profession.

Acknowledgments

I gratefully acknowledge Mr. Val Zemitis, Radiation Protection Specialist from the California Department of Health Services, Radiologic Health Branch, for his guidance with the laws relating to fluoroscopic operation and safety. His support and advice was critical in the preparation of this manuscript.

Robert Parelli
Professor, Radiology Science
Cypress College

Author

Robert J. Parelli, M.A., R.T.(R), has been the Program Director of the Department of Radiologic Technology at Cypress College since 1985 and has been an educator for 17 years. He has also served as the Radiology Department Manager at Los Alamitos Medical Center, Los Alamitos, California, and the Radiology Department Manager at Mercy General Hospital, Santa Ana, California. A former chairperson of the Education Committee, California Society of Radiologic Technologists, Mr. Parelli received his M.A. degree in Education from California State University, Long Beach, California, and his R.T. certificate from St. Mary's Medical Center, Long Beach, California. Currently, he is an active member in the American Society of Radiologic Technologists, the California Society of Radiologic Technologists, and the Association of Educators in Radiology Sciences.

© GR/St. Lucie Press

Chapter 1

Image Intensifier System

Objectives

Upon completion of Chapter 1, the reader will be able to:

1. Describe the basic parts of the image intensifier tube: input phosphor and photocathode, electrostatic lens, accelerating anode, and output phosphor.
2. Explain how to use a dual field image intensifier tube for magnification procedures.
3. Calculate the amount of patient exposure in the magnified mode.
4. Define conversion factor and brightness gain.
5. Calculate the minification ratio of the image intensifier tube.
6. Explain how image quality of the image intensifier tube is affected by scintillation, resolution, contrast, and distortion.
7. Describe the automatic brightness stabilizer system.
8. Recall the types of brightness sensing devices.
9. Identify the types of automatic brightness sensing circuits that are used with the x-ray generator.

© GR/St. Lucie Press

Conventional fluoroscopy, without image intensification, has two serious limitations: it produces a statistically inferior image and one too dim for photopic (daylight) vision. In the early 1950s, the x-ray image intensifier was developed, which has revolutionized fluoroscopy. Its image is bright enough for scotopic vision and small enough to be conveniently coupled to cine, television, or spot-film cameras.

Image Intensifier Tube Design

The image intensifier tube is an evacuated glass envelope, a vacuum tube, which contains four basic parts (Figure 1.1):

1. Input phosphor and photocathode.
2. Electrostatic focusing lens.
3. Accelerating anode.
4. Output phosphor.

Input Phosphor and Photocathode

First-generation image intensifier tubes had silver-activated zinc cadmium sulfide crystals in the input screen. Second-generation intensifiers have cesium iodide (CsI) input screens. The fluorescent material is deposited on a thin substrate of the glass envelope. It serves the purpose of converting incident x-ray beam photons into a light image. The fluorescent screen and the photocathode are separated by a thin transparent layer only a fraction of a millimeter. Very little of the image is lost as the image is transferred from the screen to the photocathode.

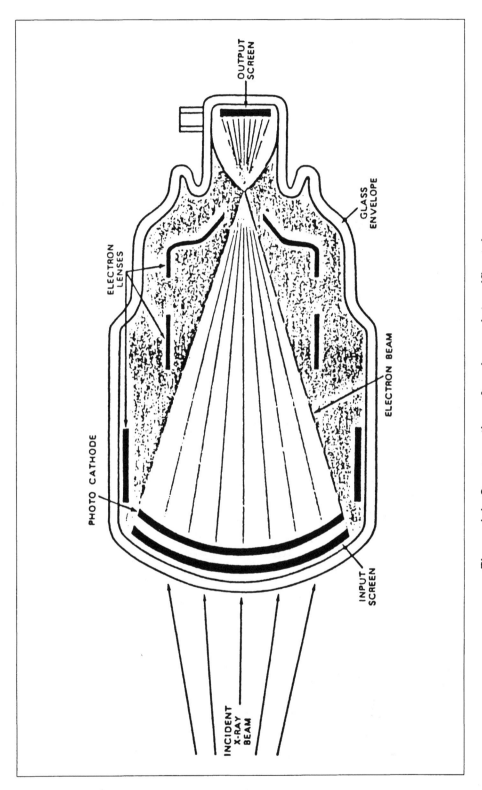

Figure 1.1: Cross-section of an image intensifier tube.

The **photocathode** is a photo-emissive metal (usually a combination of antimony [Sb] and cesium [Cs] compounds). The photocathode receives the light emitted from the input screen and emits electrons in proportion to the intensity of the light it receives. One can appreciate the necessity of the input screen and photocathode being in very close proximity. Otherwise the image detail transmitted from one to the other would be significantly degraded. The photocathode also serves as the cathode of the image intensifier tube. It is kept at ground potential. By establishing a voltage or difference in electrical potential between the cathode and the accelerating anode, the electrons can be made to transverse the tube toward the output screen.

Electrostatic Focusing Lens

The focusing of electrons is accomplished by a series of rings called the electrostatic lenses, which are located inside the tube envelope and concentric with the tube axis. Applying a positive electrical potential difference to the electrostatic lens will cause the electrons emitted from the photocathode to be focused into an extremely fine beam. Each point on the input screen is focused to a specific point on the opposite side of the output screen. Electron focusing inverts the image on the output phosphor. The image on the output phosphor is reduced in size, which is one of the principal reasons why it is brighter.

Accelerating Anode

Located at the neck of the image intensifier tube, the accelerating anode draws electrons from the photocathode and accelerates them toward the output screen. The anode of a 6-in. image intensifier tube has a positive potential difference (voltage) of 25,000 volts (25 kVp), so it accelerates electrons to a tremendous velocity.

Output Phosphor

The output fluorescent screen of the 6-in. image intensifier tube is made from cesium iodide. The crystal size and layer thickness are reduced to maintain resolution in the minified image. Since the electrons are greatly accelerated, they emit more light photons from the output screen than were originally present in the input screen. The number of light photons is increased approximately 50 times. A thin layer of aluminum is plated onto the fluorescent screen to prevent light from moving retrograde through the tube and activating the photocathode. The aluminum layer is very thin, and high-energy photoelectrons easily pass through it en route to the output screen. This layer also serves as a ground to remove spent electrons from the image tube. If they were not removed, they would accumulate on the output phosphor and build up a negative charge.

The output screen is optically coupled to a viewing system by subjective lenses. The image is viewed either directly through a series of lenses and mirrors or indirectly through a closed circuit television system.

Dual Field Image Intensifier Tubes

Field size on the output phosphor is changed by applying a simple electronic principle: the higher the voltage on the electrostatic focusing lens, the more the electron

© GR/St. Lucie Press

beam is focused. Figure 1.2 shows this principle applied to a dual field image intensifier.

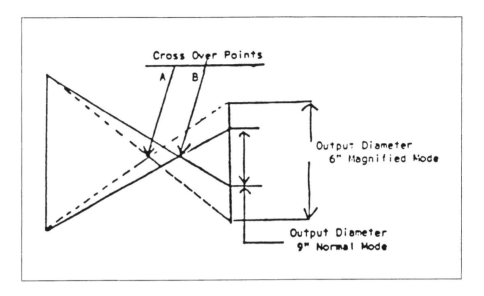

Figure 1.2: Dual field image intensifier.

In the 9-in. mode, the electrostatic focusing voltage is decreased. The electrons focus to a point, or cross, close to the output phosphor, and the image is actually smaller than the phosphor. In the 6-in. mode, the electrostatic focusing voltage is increased, and the electrons focus farther away from the output phosphor. After the electrons cross, they diverge so the image on the output screen is larger than the 9-in. mode. The physical size of the input and output screens is the same in both modes; the only thing that changes is the size of the output image. Therefore, the 6- and 9-in. modes have different minification gains. Exposure factors are automatically increased when the unit is used in the magnified mode to compensate for the decreased brightness from minification. The ratio of patient exposure is calculated using this formula:

$$\frac{(\text{Normal mode size})^2}{(\text{Magnified mode size})^2} = \text{Increase in patient exposure}$$

Example: When operating the image intensifier in the magnified 6-in. mode from the normal 9-in. mode, the patient will receive how many times more exposure?

Answer:
$$\frac{(9)^2}{(6)^2} = 2.25 \text{ times more exposure}$$

It is important to note that the normal mode is always used to view larger anatomic areas with less patient exposure. When size is unimportant, the magnified mode is used for better resultant image quality. *The mA is automatically increased when the unit is used in the 6-in. magnified mode to compensate for the decreased brightness. Therefore, patient dose is increased.*

Conversion Factor and Gain

When x-ray image intensifier tubes were first introduced, some means was needed to express their increased intensity. Because of the past familiarity with conventional fluoroscopic screens, it became commonplace to compare the image intensifier tube to the screen. The **brightness gain,** or "intensification gain" as it was called, was then expressed as the luminance of the output screen compared to the luminance of a standard Patterson fluoroscopic screen with the same incident radiation. The brightness gain is the ratio of the two illuminations:

$$\text{Brightness gain} = \frac{\text{Intensifier luminance}}{\text{Patterson B-2 luminance}}$$

The first image tubes that gained widespread acceptance had gains on the order of 3,000 or possibly a little higher. As improvements in design and manufacturing came along, this gain gradually moved upward into the area of 4,000 to 5,000.

Principles of Fluoroscopic Image Intensification and Television Systems: Workbook and Laboratory Manual

This method of measuring gain did have some drawbacks: brightness gain measurements were not reproducible, and there was no way of knowing whether the intensifier tube or the fluorescent screen was deteriorated. The International Commission on Radiologic Units and Measurements (ICRU) has recommended a second method of evaluation called the conversion factor. The **conversion factor** is a ratio of the luminance of the output phosphor to the input exposure rate:

$$\text{Conversion Factor} = \frac{cd/m^2}{mR/sec}$$

$$cd = candelas$$

Radiation quality and output luminance are explicitly defined so the method is accurate and reproducible.

Brightness gain tends to deteriorate as the image intensifier ages. This means that the patient dose with an old image intensifier tends to be higher than one with a new intensifier of the same type. Deterioration rate can proceed at a rate of 10% per year; therefore, a periodic check of image intensifier brightness is important.

The brightness gain of an image intensifier tube comes from two completely unrelated sources called **minification gain** and **flux gain**.

Flux Gain

For each light photon emitted from the input screen of the image intensifier tube, on the average, 50 light photons are emitted on the output phosphor screen. Remember that one light photon from the input screen will eject one electron from the photocathode. This one electron will have enough kinetic energy to produce 50 light photons at the output screen. It is important to understand that the flux gain is an inherent number that each individual image intensifier tube manufacturer will indicate.

Minification Gain

The brightness gain from minification is produced by a reduction in image size. The quantity of the gain depends on the relative areas of the input and output screens. Because the size of an intensifier is usually indicated by its diameter, it is more convenient to express minification gain in terms of diameter:

$$\text{Minification gain} = \frac{(d_1)^2}{(d_0)^2}$$

d_1 = diameter of the input screen
d_0 = diameter of the output screen

Image intensifier input screen size varies from 6, 9, 10, 12, or 14 in., whereas the output screen size has an approximately 1-in. diameter.

Example: What is the minification ratio of a 9-in. image intensification tube?

Answer:
$$\frac{(9)^2}{(1)^2} = 81$$

The brightness gain from minification does not improve the statistical quality of the fluoroscopic image. The total brightness gain of an image intensifier is the product of the minification and flux gains:

$$\text{Brightness gain} = \text{minification gain} \times \text{flux gain}$$

For example, with a flux gain of 50 and a minification gain of 81, the total brightness gain is 4,050 (50 $\times$ 81). Brightness gain from modern image intensifiers is always over 1,000 and frequently as high as 6,000.

Image Quality

The number of absorbed x-ray photons determines the highest possible statistical quality of an imaging system. No form of intensification can improve the image above the statistical level of the absorbed photons. Image quality of the image intensifier system is affected by **scintillation**, **resolution**, **contrast**, and **distortion**.

Scintillation

This effect is known by many names. Sometimes it is called **quantum noise**, sometimes **quantum mottle**, and sometimes **scintillation**. As viewed in the final fluoroscopic display, the effect will be something like a random noise pattern superimposed on the fluoroscopic image. This noise pattern, since it is random in nature, has a tendency to appear to be moving, giving rise to the colloquial expression "crawling ants." This effect occurs when an insufficient number of x-ray quanta per unit of time is absorbed in the input screen. Quantum noise/quantum mottle can be improved by a higher x-ray-to-light conversion efficiency, but quality can never be raised above that of the absorbed photons. Therefore, the usual method employed to eliminate quantum noise is to raise the x-ray tube current, thus generating more x-ray quanta in a given period of time. Once this threshold is reached, the noise disappears, and the fluoroscopic display takes on a much more pleasing appearance and is generally easier to interpret.

Another way to increase the number of absorbed photons is by capturing a higher percentage of the incident x-ray beam. Cesium iodide image intensifier tubes capture a greater percentage of the incident beam than the silver-activated zinc cadmium sulfide screens, so statistical quality is superior for any given level of exposure.

Resolution

An important consideration of an image intensifier tube is that of its resolving power capability or resolution. This is usually expressed in line pairs per inch or line pairs per millimeter, which is in keeping with the photographic means of expressing resolution. A **line pair** is defined to consist of a line plus an adjacent space of equivalent width such that, for example, two of them will fit into a space 1 mm wide; then, it is considered to be 2 line pairs/mm. The resolution of zinc cadmium sulfide image tubes is 1–2 line pairs per millimeter (lp/mm). The resolution of cesium iodide image tubes is approximately 4 lp/mm, a dramatic improvement over zinc cadmium sulfide. The individual cesium iodide crystals are somewhat aligned, and the phosphor layer is thinner, both contributing to improved resolution.

The primary limitation to resolving power in an image intensifier tube is the input screen. The manufacturer must make a decision as to the trade-off between resolution and gain in formulating this input screen. To make the input screen of thinner or finer grained phosphors will increase resolution but will decrease gain. Conversely, using a thicker screen or a large particle size will increase gain at the expense of resolution. The output screen does contribute slightly to further loss of resolution, as is evidenced by the approximately 10% improvement realized in the dual field tube by distributing a given number of lines at the input. A somewhat larger diameter at the output screen would have little, if any, further improvement in resolution.

Contrast

One of the areas in which the image intensifier tube does not perform well is in the area of **contrast**. The contrast in the final image at the output screen is lowered by one or more various effects. Any x-ray quanta incident on the input screen which is not absorbed by the input screen would pass through the intensifier tube and, if close to the intensifier tube axis, would strike the output screen. Since this x-ray quanta has a property of exciting the output screen if it is absorbed, it will cause the output screen to fluoresce and thus produce an overall masking effect or a type of inverse fog on the screen itself. More specifically, any light emitted backwards from the output screen strikes the photocathode, causing it to emit additional electrons. These electrons are in a random pattern and are not part of the original image but are focused and accelerated onto the output screen just like those that originated from the primary x-ray beam. Contrast tends to deteriorate as an image intensifier ages.

Distortion

In the present state of development, electron focusing is not uniform across the entire width of an image intensifier. Electrons at the center of the unit are more accurately focused than those at the periphery. Peripheral electrons tend to flare out from an ideal course. The result is unequal magnification, which produces peripheral distortion. The amount of distortion is greater with larger intensifiers because the further an electron is from the center of the intensifier, the more difficult it is to focus. Unequal magnification also causes unequal illumination. The center of the output screen is brighter than the periphery. The peripheral image is displayed over a larger area of the output screen, and, thus, its brightness gain from minification is less than that in the center. A decrease in brightness at the periphery of an image is called **vignetting**. Unequal focusing has another effect on image quality; resolution is better in the center of the screen.

Pincushion distortion is a form of spatial distortion that warps the appearance of the image. It is a consequence of projecting the image formed on a curved input phosphor to a flat output phosphor. Pincushion distortion results in slightly higher magnification of the input image toward the edge of the image. The amount of pincushion distortion is usually determined by an imaging grid or screen with regular rectangular spacing.

Pincushion distortion is a result of the curved surface of the input phosphor and a flat surface of the output phosphor. This results in a warped image. Pincushion distortion is reduced when magnification modes are used.

Veiling glare is mainly the consequence of light scatter in the output window of the image intensifier. The scattered light, just like scattered radiation, adds to the background signal and reduces the contrast in the image. Veiling glare can be reduced by purchasing an image intensifier with an advanced output window design. There is not much that can be done about the presence of veiling glare.

In summary, the center of the image intensifier screen has

1. Better resolution.
2. A brighter image.
3. Less geometric distortion.

Automatic Brightness Stabilization

The automatic brightness stabilizer (ABS) is that part of the fluoroscopic control system which keeps the light output of the image intensifier constant over variations of patient attenuation and system geometry. Portions of the system may be shared with automatic exposure control systems that maintain constant film density of cineradiographic or fluoroscopic spot films. A properly designed ABS system must accomplish the following objectives:

1. It must hold the image brightness constant for variations of patient thickness and attenuation.
2. It must ignore information at the image margins.
3. It must operate to preserve image contrast and minimize image noise.
4. It must keep the operation within the ratings of the x-ray tube.
5. It must effect a reasonable compromise between patient exposure and image quality.
6. It must keep the patient exposure within the California Radiation Control Regulations of 10 R/min., except when an override mode of operation is selected by the operator (5 R/min.).
7. It must respond quickly enough to track during an examination but slowly enough to avoid hunting between bright and dark portions of the image.
8. It must compensate for system variables such as the magnification of the image, the intensifier, and the use of disc recorders.
9. It must be capable of being disabled or "held" at a particular equilibrium value prior to injection of contrast media.
10. It must be capable of being shut off to permit the manual control of factors.
11. It must display the operating factors and modes of operation to the operator.

Variations with X-ray Factors

Operation of the system at higher kVp values will result in increased transmission of the beam by the patient so that less radiation is required. The brightness of the image varies directly as mA and as the fifth power of kVp. Thus, as the kVp would vary from 80 to 88 kVp, a 10% change, there would be a 50% change of brightness.

It is important to note that contrast degrades as kVp is increased. Therefore, the ABS should operate at high values for reduced patient exposure and at low values of kVp for best image contrast. When viewing low-contrast objects in fluoroscopy, the system should be operated at the lower kVp values. This is particularly true when using iodine-based contrast media as in cholecystography, arthrography, and arteriography.

More specifically, when examining the gastrointestinal tract, particularly when using barium-based contrast media, operation at high kVp is better. The images are of fairly high contrast, and patient exposure is reduced.

Brightness Sensing

Image brightness can be sensed in several ways:

1. **Image Intensifier Photocathode Current.** The photocathode of the image intensifier is normally connected to ground, and the final anode of the tube connected can be removed and fed to a current amplifier so that the amplifier output is proportional to the radiation input to the intensifying tube.

2. **Television Camera Signal Sensing.** Most television cameras have automatic gain control (AGC) circuits for controlling the camera tube target voltage or the gain in video amplifiers in order to provide a constant output signal over variations of image brightness. The AGC can be used to control the generator as well.

3. **Lens-Coupled Photo Tube Sensing.** This method uses a lens often combined with a prism or mirror, so that the collimated light from the image intensifier is sampled, and the image of the output phosphor is formed over an aperture plate in front of a photomultiplier tube. This system will compensate for coning effects, field size changes, and mode changes of the image intensifier tube and will ignore bright flashes at the margin. The gain of the photomulti-

plier tube can be controlled by adjustment of its power supply voltage so that it may be shared between fluoroscopic ABS circuits and the various filming systems.

Types of ABS Stabilization Circuits

Brightness stabilizers can be classified in terms of the variable controlled by the brightness sensor.

1. **Variable mA, preset kVp.** In this system, the operator presents the kVp, and the brightness sensor controls the tube current over a range of about 20 to 1. The operator can set this system to the kVp required for the particular examination, and the brightness sensor will automatically adjust the mA to yield an image of contrast brightness.

2. **Variable mA with kVp following.** This system operates by varying the mA as a function of the brightness sensor, but it has an additional circuit that senses if an upper- or lower-bound mA has been exceeded and then controls the adjustment of kVp through a motor-driven variable transformer. Therefore, if the mA rises above a certain preset value, then the motor will drive the kVp value higher.

3. **Variable kVp with selected mA.** In this system, the brightness sensor controls the kVp of the system. The operator will have previously selected the value of mA required. If a motor-driven variable transformer is used to select kVp, the system has the additional advantage of remembering the last operating point as the operator energizes the system with the foot switch; thus, restabilization of the system between scenes is very rapid. The operator can select a low mA, which will force the brightness stabilizer to operate at a higher kVp for gastrointestinal examinations, or a high mA, which will force the kVp of the system downward for best contrast when viewing iodine-based contrast media.

4. **Variable kVp, variable mA.** In this system, the output of the brightness sensor controls both kVp and mA in order to maintain either constant image noise or constant image contrast. Unfortunately, such systems make it difficult for the operator to select the mode of operation best suited for the particular examination.

Review Questions

1. The four basic parts of the image intensifier tube are

   a.

   b.

   c.

   d.

2. The input phosphor of a recent image intensification tube has _____ fluorescent screens.

3. A photocathode is a device that emits

   a. photons.

   b. light photons.

   c. electrons.

   d. thermions.

4. The photocathode also serves as a _____ and is kept at ground potential.

5. Focusing of the electrons in the image intensifier tube is accomplished by the _____.

6. The potential difference of the accelerating anode is

   a. 25 volts.

   b. 250 volts.

   c. 250 kV.

   d. 25 kV.

7. The output screen is optically coupled to a viewing system by _____ _____.

8. The ICRU has recommended the _____ as a method of evaluating gain.

9. Output screen luminance is measured in

   a. lamberts.

   b. millilamberts.

   c. candela.

   d. quanta.

10. Brightness gain of an image intensifier comes from two unrelated sources called _____ gain and _____ gain.

11. What is the minification ratio if the input phosphor size is 30.5 cm and the output phosphor size is 2.54 cm?

12. Before the bright image from the output phosphor can be viewed, it must be

    a.   refracted.

    b.   magnified.

    c.   reflected.

    d.   accelerated.

13. A brightness gain of approximately _____ will satisfy light requirements for photopic vision.

14. The statistical quality of the image can be improved by

    a.   increasing the x-ray beam.

    b.   increasing the tube current.

    c.   increasing the quantity of the incident photon.

    d.   increasing the x-ray-to-light conversion efficiency.

15. Contrast will diminish as quantum mottle increases, causing illumination of the output phosphor, but does not contribute to

    a.   brightness level.

    b.   image formation.

    c.   minification.

    d.   flux gain.

16. Contrast will diminish with retrograde electron flow from the _____ _____.

17. In the magnified mode of operation, the electron focal point is _____ from the output phosphor.

18. A reduction of brightness at the periphery of the image is referred to as _____.

19. In the magnified mode, the voltage supplied to the accelerating anode is

    a.   increased.

    b.   decreased.

    c.   remains the same.

20. In fluoroscopic units with automatic exposure control, the exposure factors will automatically _____ in the magnified mode.

■ Principles of Fluoroscopic Image Intensification and Television Systems: Workbook and Laboratory Manual

21. To increase the resolution of the image intensifier tube, the input screen phosphors must be
    a. thinner.
    b. thicker.
    c. coarse.
    d. none of the above.

22. Brightness gain will increase when the input phosphors are
    a. thinner.
    b. thicker.
    c. coarse.
    d. none of the above.

23. With fluoroscopic systems equipped with automatic exposure control (ABS) mechanisms and where the x-ray tube is fixed below the table, moving the image intensifier away from the patient will
    a. reduce the image size.
    b. increase the patient dose.
    c. decrease the patient dose.
    d. increase the size of the radiation field at the table top.

24. The central portion of the image intensifier tube possesses the greatest
    a. detail.
    b. aberration.
    c. brightness.
    d. resolution.

25. An image-intensified fluoroscopy system is switched to the magnification mode so that the center 6 in. of the input screen is now visualized over the entire 9-in. diameter input screen. Under automatic brightness control with constant kVp, what relative increase in exposure rate has occurred?

Answers to the review questions are on page 177. If you answered 18 or more items correctly, go to the next chapter. If you answered fewer than 18 items correctly, reread the chapter and retake the review questions.

© GR/St. Lucie Press

Chapter 2

Objective and Camera Lenses

Objectives

Upon completion of Chapter 2, the reader will be able to:

1. Describe the basic optical design for the image intensifier viewing system.
2. Define focal length, relative aperture, and field of view.
3. Define real and virtual images.
4. Recall integration time.
5. Explain motion integration time.

Optics

The basic optics for an image-intensified viewing system consist of an objective lens and a camera lens. Figure 2.1 graphically shows the action of the objective or collimating lens system. Note that the objective lens collects light emanating from the output screen of the image intensifier tube and projects it into a large single-element lens, which then creates the real image. The primary reason for dividing the objective lens into two parts is to establish parallel light between them. In most systems, it is

© GR/St. Lucie Press

21

possible to swing a small elliptical mirror or beam splitter into place between these two elements and direct a portion of the light into a cine, 70mm, or closed circuit television camera.

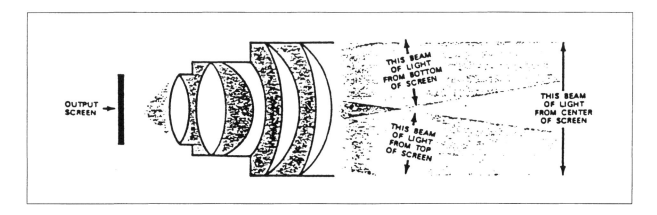

Figure 2.1: Intensifier objective lens.

There are three primary characteristics for which any lens is designed, aside from the overall quality and performance level necessary for the particular application. These three are **focal length**, **relative aperture** (or speed as it is usually known), and **field of view**.

Focal Length

In a simple lens, focal length is usually of most importance. This is a characteristic of all lenses and is generally used to identify a lens since it is a measure of the refracting power of the lens. **Refraction** is defined as the bending of a beam of light energy when it passes across an interface of materials with different indices of refraction. **Focal length** is simply the distance measured from the lens to a focal point. The **focal point** is, by definition, that point at which light incident upon a lens from an infinitely distant object is brought to a focus. The importance of focal length lies in the fact that this is the determining factor in the magnification at which a scene is an image on the television camera tube. Lens characteristics are shown in Figure 2.2

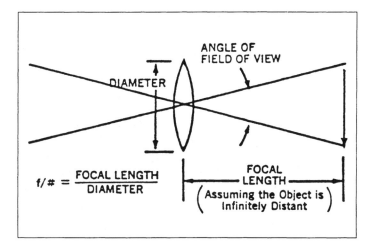

Figure 2.2: Lens characteristics.

Relative Aperture

Although **relative aperture** is the correct technical term, the much more common term used to describe this characteristic of a lens is called **speed**. Basically this has to do with the light-gathering ability of the lens and is of most importance in photographic systems in determining the amount of exposure necessary to produce a negative of the correct density. As any camera fan knows, this is usually referred to as the "f" number. It is a dimensionless number expressing the ratio of the focal length divided by the diameter of the entrance of the pupil of the lens. Figure 2.3 illustrates this characteristic. The definition of aperture ratio, or the f/number, can be expressed mathematically as

$$\text{f/number} = \frac{\text{Focal length}}{\text{diameter}}$$

■ Principles of Fluoroscopic Image Intensification and Television Systems: Workbook and Laboratory Manual

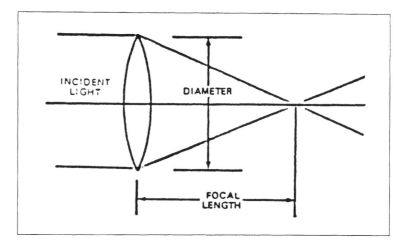

Figure 2.3: f/number of a lens.

For the sake of standardization, the American Standards Association has suggested that certain fixed f/numbers be marked on photographic lenses. The progression usually is as follows: 0.7, 1.0, 1.4, 2.0, 2.8, 4.0, 5.6, 8.0, 11.0, 16.0, and 22. Inspection of this progression will reveal that each successively higher number is approximately 1.4 times the previous number. The 1.4 progression factor mentioned is the square root of two. As we move upward in this progression, **if the focal length is kept fixed**, the change in f/number means that the diameter is decreasing by a factor of 1.4 each time. Since the area is equivalent to the square of this change in diameter and $1.4^2 = 2$, it means that each successive number will require an exposure time twice as long (i.e., if the correct exposure time with the lens set at f4 was 0.5 sec., with the lens stopped down to f5.6, the correct exposure time would be 1 sec. If the lens is being opened up from f4 to f2.8, the required exposure time is only half as long, then being 0.5 sec.

Field of View

The last subject to be covered in our study of lens characteristics has to do with the **field of view**. This has to do with a maximum area over which the lens is capable of producing a usable image. Photographic lenses are usually designed for some particular format such as 16mm cine, 35mm still, or even larger. The field of view of the lens does not necessarily dictate the lens diameter. One can have large aperture lenses for small fields or vice versa. Lenses to be used with diagnostic television equipment usually fall into one of two categories. Vidicon pick-up tubes have a sensitive target of 0.375 by 0.50 in. and lenses used with the vidicon are sometimes those designed for use with 16mm cine cameras. The standard 16mm format is 0.294 in. by 0.410 in., and since a vidicon is only slightly larger, 16mm camera lenses will often suffice. Larger pick-up tubes having larger target areas require lenses designed to cover larger fields of view. Some may be used for 35mm cine formats and double frame 35-frame formats.

Real and Virtual Images

Discussion, to this point, has dealt with **real images** (i.e., images created by the actual intersection of light rays). If a piece of diffusing material, such as ground glass (lens), is placed in the plane of the image, it can be made visible. This real image is a necessary requirement of any photographic system in which the image must be displayed on film. In certain optical instruments, there is a second class of images called **virtual images**. A virtual image cannot be projected onto a diffusing screen but exists only for computational purposes and is used for calculating magnification and subsequent image position. The ordinary magnifying glass produces an example of a virtual image.

Magnifiers are frequently combined with other lenses in various optical systems (Figure 2.4). In image intensification, most mirror-viewing systems create at least one virtual image in the course of the light rays traversing the system.

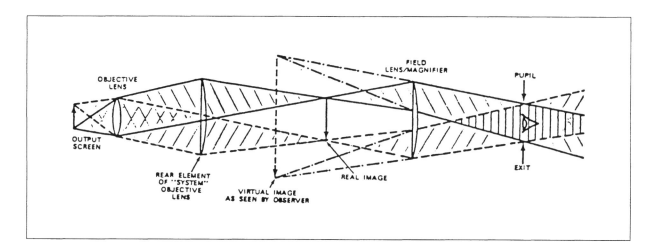

Figure 2.4: Real and virtual images.

Review Questions

1. An image created by the actual intersection of light rays is called
   a. virtual image.
   b. real image.
   c. magnified image.
   d. prism.

2. The focal length of a lens is the distance measured from the lens to a
   _____.

3. The _____ has to do with the light gathering ability of the lens.

4. Doubling the aperture of the lens would _____ its light gathering ability.

5. Images that exist for computational purposes, magnification, and/or image position are referred to as
   a. virtual images.
   b. real images.
   c. diffused images.
   d. mirrored images.

6. If the output intensity of the x-ray tube is 240 mR/hr. at 2 mA of tube current, what would be the intensity at 5 mA of tube current?

Answers to the review questions are on page 177. If you answered 4 or more items correctly, go to the next chapter. If you answered fewer than 4 items correctly, reread the chapter and retake the review questions.

© GR/St. Lucie Press

Chapter 3

Closed Circuit Television Systems

Objectives

Upon completion of Chapter 3, the reader will be able to:

1. Describe the target assembly of the vidicon camera pick-up tube.
2. Explain how the video signal is produced.
3. Define a television frame.
4. Recall the purpose of interlaced horizontal scanning.
5. Define bandwidth/bandpass.
6. Use the camera control unit.
7. Describe synchronization.
8. Identify the basic parts of the picture tube or kinescope.
9. Explain how horizontal resolution, vertical resolution, contrast, and brightness have an effect on the quality of the television image.
10. Define lag.
11. Compare and contrast the plumbicon and image-orthocon cameras.
12. Calculate the Kell factor.

Camera Pick-Up Tubes

Fluoroscopic television systems are always closed circuit systems. The video signal is transmitted from one component to the next through cables rather than through the air as in broadcast television. A lens system, which has been discussed in the previous section, conveys the fluoroscopic image from the output phosphor of the image intensifier to the video camera, where it is converted into a series of video signals. This signal is transmitted through the cable to the camera control unit, where it is amplified and then forwarded through another cable to the television monitor.

The television image is made up of a mosaic of hundreds of thousands of tiny dots with different brightness, each contributing a minute bit to the total picture. At close range, the dots are clearly visible. The dot distribution is not random or haphazard; instead, the dots are arranged in a specific pattern along horizontal lines called **horizontal scan lines**. Most fluoroscopic television systems use a 525-scan-line system.

The vidicon camera is the one usually employed for fluoroscopy. It is a relatively inexpensive, compact unit (5-in. diameter, 9-in. length) that weighs approximately 6 lbs. The essential parts of the vidicon camera are shown in Figure 3.1. The most important part is the vidicon tube, a small electronic vacuum tube with a 1-in. diameter and 2-in. length.

The tube is surrounded by two pairs of coils: (1) the electromagnetic focusing coils and (2) the electrostatic deflecting coils.

The image from the image intensifier is focused onto the target assembly which consists of the following three layers:

1. A glass faceplate.
2. A signal plate.
3. A target.

Chapter 3 ■ Closed Circuit Television Systems

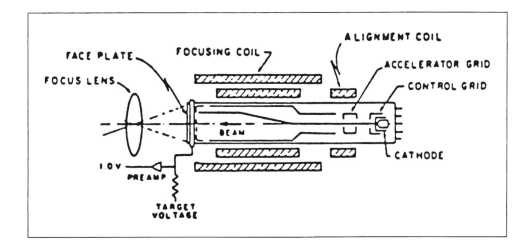

Figure 3.1: Camera tube construction.

The only function of the faceplate is to allow light to pass through the vacuum tube on its way to the target. The signal plate is a thin transparent film of graphite located on the inner surface of the faceplate. It is an electrical conductor with a positive potential difference of approximately 25 volts. The signal plate transmits the video signal.

The vidicon target is functionally the most important element in the tube. It is a thin film of photoconductive material made from antimony trisulfite suspended as globules in a mica matrix. Each globule has a diameter of 0.001 in. and is insulated from its neighbors and from the signal plate by the mica matrix. The globules form a mosaic of tiny light-sensitive elements, and they form the dot picture. The function of the globules is to act as tiny capacitors that store an electrical charge.

The cathode of the tube is located at the opposite end of the vidicon tube from the target and is heated indirectly by an internal electric coil. The cathode-heating coil is referred to as an **electron gun**. The heating coil releases electrons through the process of thermionic emission. These electrons are immediately formed into a beam by the control grid that initiates their acceleration towards the target.

The **anode** has a positive potential of approximately 250 volts with respect to the cathode, and it accelerates the electron beam to a relatively high velocity. The anode extends across the target end of the tube as a fine wire mesh. The wire mesh and signal plate form a uniform decelerating field adjacent to the target. The signal plate (+25 volts) has a potential of 225 volts less than the wire mesh (+250 volts), so electrons should flow from the signal plate to the wire mesh. The electrons from the cathode are accelerated to high velocities, but they will coast through the decelerating field like a roller coaster going uphill. When they reach the target, they have been slowed to near standstill. The decelerating field performs a second function; it straightens the final path of the electron beam so that it strikes the target perpendicularly.

Since the electron beam scans a dot picture, it must be focused to a point the size of the dots. This is accomplished by two pairs of **electromagnetic focusing coils**. These coils wrap around the vidicon tube (Figure 3.2). The coils extend the entire length of the tube and create a constant magnetic field that forces the beam of electrons into a narrow bundle. As the electrons are forced together, they will repel each other and diverge, only to be brought back together by the **focusing cell**.

The electron beam is steered by variable electrostatic fields produced by two pairs of **deflecting coils** that wrap around the vidicon tube in a manner similar to that of the focusing coil. Figure 3.2 shows the vertical deflecting coils. By alternating the current on the coils, the focused electron beam is moved up and down to scan the target. The other pair of coils moves the beam from side to side along a horizontal line. All four coils, working together, move the electron beam almost instantaneously over the target.

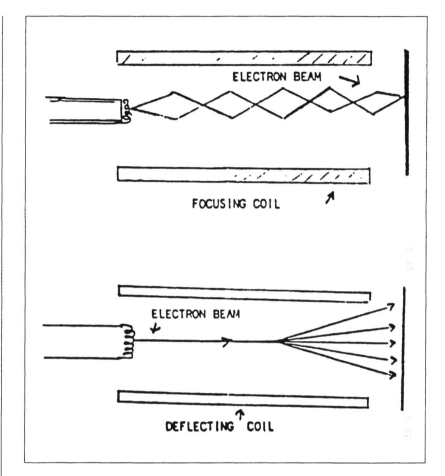

Figure 3.2: Vertical deflecting coils.

Video Signal

When a globule on the target absorbs light photons, it emits electrons. The electrons are immediately attracted to the anode and removed from the tube. The globule, having lost electrons, becomes positively charged (Figure 3.3). It is insulated from its surroundings so that it behaves like half of a tiny capacitor and draws a current into the conductive signal plate. The current that flows into the signal plate is ignored, or clipped, and is not recorded. Similar events occur over the entire surface of the target. A brighter area in the light image emits more photoelectrons than a dim area and produces a stronger charge on the tiny capacitor. The result is a mosaic of charged globules which store an electrical image that is an exact replica of the light image focused onto the target.

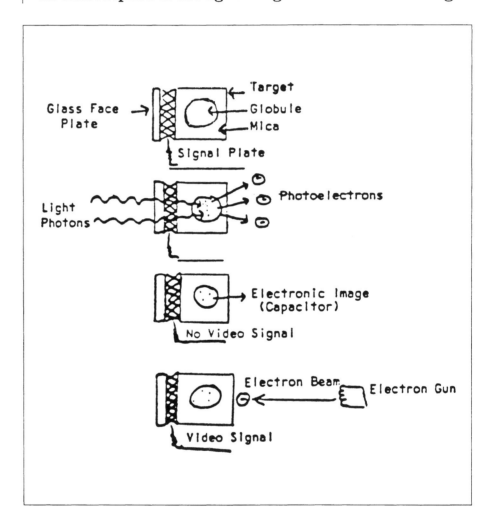

Figure 3.3: Formation of the video signal.

The electron beam scans the electrical image stored on the target and fills in the holes left by the emitted photoelectrons, thus discharging the capacitors of the tiny globule. Excess electrons from the scanning beam drift back to the anode and are removed from the tube. At the instant of discharge, a current flows through the conductive signal plate, and this current forms the video signal. The globules are not all discharged at the same time. Only a small cluster, a dot, is discharged each instant in time. Then, the electron beam moves on to the next dot in an orderly sequence but at an enormous speed. It will discharge all the globules on the target. The result is a series of video pulses, all originating from the same signal plate but separated in time. Each pulse corresponds to an exact location on the target. Reassembling these pulses back into a visible image is accomplished by the camera control unit and the television monitor.

Television Scanning System

The television image is stored as an electron image on the target of the vidicon tube and is scanned along 525 lines by a narrow electron beam 30 times/sec. Each scan of the entire target is called a **television frame**. The electron beam scans the target beginning at the top left corner; then, it drifts across a line, sending out a video signal as it moves and rapidly returns to the left margin and repeats the process over and over until all 525 lines have been read. As the beam reads, it also erases. As the electron beam discharges the globule-capacitors, it erases their image. It is then ready to record a new image, and it begins immediately. When the electron beam returns, it sees a different image than it saw the time before. Because the electron beam scans the target 30 times each second, the change in the image from one scan to the next is slight. Our eyes will perceive a continuous motion. To avoid the "flicker effect," an electronic trick called **interlaced horizontal scanning** is employed. Instead of scanning all 525 lines consecutively each frame, only the odd-numbered lines are scanned in the first half of the frame, and only the even-numbered lines are scanned during the second half. Figure 3.4 shows interlaced horizontal scanning. Each pass of the electron beam over the video target is called a **field** and consists of

© GR/St. Lucie Press

262.5 lines. Even though only 30 frames are displayed each second, they are displayed in 60 flashes of light, and flicker disappears.

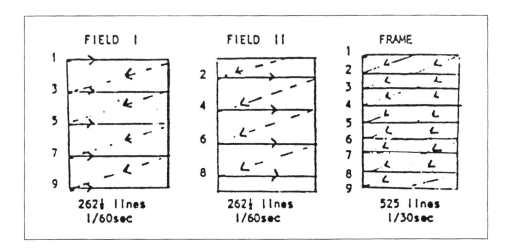

Figure 3.4: Interlaced horizontal scanning.

Video Signal Bandwidth

Bandwidth, also called bandpass, is the frequency range that the electronic components of the video system must be designed to transmit. The range from the lowest to the highest frequency is called the **bandwidth**. In the case of the television system, it defines the number of times per second that the electron beam scanning the image can be turned on and off or "modulated."

For a number of reasons such as the Federal Communications Commission regulations, consumer buying power, and the performance needed, the home television set has a bandwidth of about 3.5 megacycles per second (Mc/sec.). This means that every second, the electron beam in a receiver can be turned on and off 3.5 million times. This means there are available 3.5 million cycles of information that can be transmitted each second. The scanning process is repeated over and over 525 times per frame at 30 frames per second. The frequency of the video signal will fluctuate between a minimum of 15,750 hertz (Hz) and a maximum of 4,130,000 Hz. To transmit the signal accurately, the electronic components should have a bandpass of 4.13 to 0.015 MHz, or approximately 4.1 MHz. A little higher bandpass is required. About 10% of the scan time is lost in retracing from one line to another. This additional 10% increases the required bandpass to approximately 4.5 MHz for a 525-line system. At this bandpass, vertical and horizontal resolutions are equal. Figure 3.5 shows how the lowest and highest video signals are calculated.

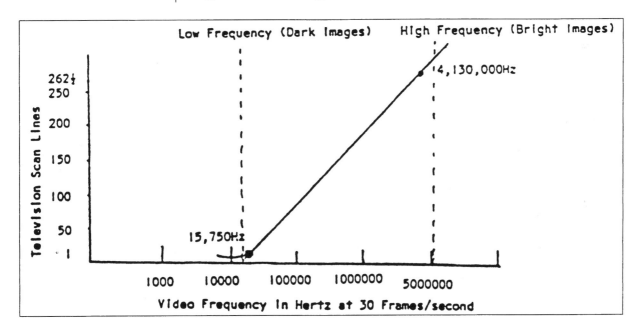

Figure 3.5: The lowest and highest video signal frequencies.

Camera Control Unit

The power supply and all the controls that regulate the camera are located within the camera control unit. It amplifies the video signal, regulates the focusing and deflecting coils, and synchronizes the video signal between the camera and monitor.

Synchronization

It is necessary to synchronize or coordinate the video signal between the camera and monitor. The camera control unit adds synchronization pulses to the video signal at the end of each scan line and scan field. These are called **horizontal** and **vertical synchronization pulses**. They are generated during the retrace time of the electronic beam while no video signal is being transmitted. First, the picture screen is blackened by a blanking pulse. If the synchronization pulses were added to the video signal while the screen was white, they would generate noise in the form of white streaks, but no visible noise is produced by synchronization on a black screen.

Note in Figure 3.6 that there is a ready-made place to insert a synchronizing pulse. At the completion of one active line, the beam must be driven to black level for some period of time in order to retrace in preparation for the next active line. The logical place for a synchronized pulse is to insert an additional signal below the black level. This additional portion of the signal is referred to as the synch pulse.

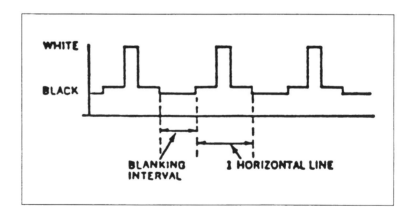

Figure 3.6: Video signal with blanking.

The blanking interval will tell the receiver, or monitor, as the case may be, to begin the retrace. At the completion of this signal level, when the signal rises to the black level, the next active line begins. The final composite video signal appears as shown in Figure 3.7.

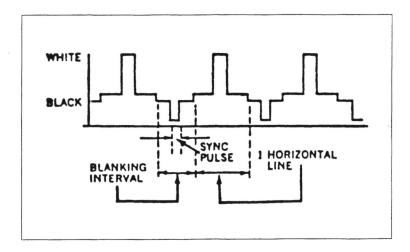

Figure 3.7: Composite video signal.

Television Monitor

The picture tube, or kinescope, will display the final image for the observer. A picture tube is very similar to a vidicon camera tube (Figure 3.8). The picture tube is made in a variety of sizes; the most common in fluoroscopy is the 14 in. with 17 in. diagonal measurement. The picture tube is a large evacuated glass tube containing a fluorescent phosphor on the inside of the faceplate and an electron gun in the neck of the tube. As in the case of the pick-up tubes, there are electrical coils around the neck of the kinescope that provide horizontal and vertical deflection of the electronic beam.

■ Principles of Fluoroscopic Image Intensification and Television Systems: Workbook and Laboratory Manual

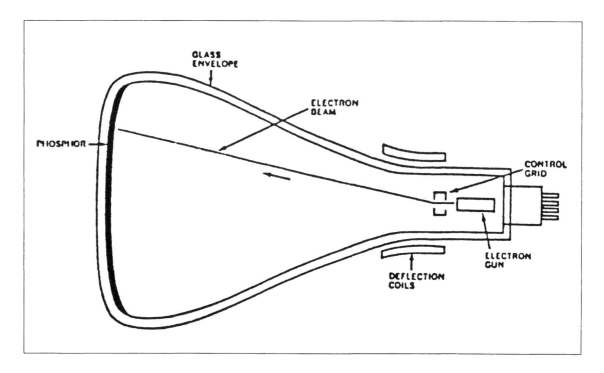

Figure 3.8: Monitor kinescope.

The brightness of the individual dots in the picture is regulated by the control grid. It receives the video signal from the television camera and uses this signal to regulate the number of electrons in the electron beam. To produce a bright area in the television picture, it allows a large number of electrons to reach the fluorescent screen. To produce a dark area, it cuts off the electron flow almost completely.

The electrons strike the fluorescent screen at the flared end of the tube and emit a large number of light photons that form the visible television image. The intensity of the light emitted by the fluorescent phosphor of the picture tube is directly proportional to the incoming signal from the camera tube. All the time that this electron beam is being modulated, it is being deflected back and forth and up and down, synchronized to the same movements in the camera pick-up tube. As the fluoroscopist observes the monitor screen, an exact reproduction of considerable magnification of the output screen of the image intensifier is displayed.

Chapter 3 ▪ Closed Circuit Television Systems

Television Image Quality

Television image quality is affected by the number of scan lines and the bandpass of the system. More specifically, horizontal resolution, vertical resolution, contrast, and brightness have an effect on the quality of the television image.

Horizontal Resolution

Bandwidth, or bandpass, refers to the total number of cycles available per second in the television camera and monitor electronics. This number will set an overall limit to the resolving power capability of the camera.

Horizontal resolution is defined as the ability to resolve vertical lines. Increasing the bandwidth will allow the television camera pick-up tube to turn on and off more times per second. The concern here is not what we are able to record and reproduce, but what we are able to display in real time.

In the 525-scan-line, 4.5-MHz television system, the amount of cycles/sec. to image one active line is approximately 803 cycles/line. If the bandpass were increased to 15 MHz with the same 525 scan lines, the frequency to image one active line would be approximately 2,671 cycles/line.

Frequency per line is a measure of horizontal resolving power of the camera pick-up tube and monitor. Therefore, more information is gained as the bandwidth is increased.

Vertical Resolution

Vertical resolving power is the ability of a television system to resolve horizontal lines. One way to improve

© GR/St. Lucie Press

41

television resolution is with more and smaller dots, or target globules, which means more scan lines.

Contrast

The camera and television monitor will affect the contrast of the television image. Contrast levels can be adjusted on the television monitor.

The contrast should be set so that the darkest object in the scene is just below the black level on the monitor and the bright objects of interest do not completely saturate or "white out" such that details in the image are lost. It is appropriate when viewing contrast within the patient to adjust the contrast and brightness controls to maximize the visibility of the object even at the expense of increased noise.

Brightness

Changes in image brightness will seriously affect the television image quality. When the fluoroscope is moved from the abdomen to the chest, a sudden surge of brightness floods the system, the image becomes chalky, and all detail is lost. Therefore, the brightness level of the television monitor must be controlled within narrow limits. Usually the automatic brightness control will stabilize the bright image and the x-ray exposure factors.

It is important to remember that the brightness level of the television monitor can be increased indefinitely, but this does not improve image quality. Usually brightness and contrast are adjusted in combination. Contrast is brought to near maximum level, and brightness is adjusted to produce a satisfactory level of illumination.

Lag

An undesirable property of most vidicon camera tubes is **lag**. Lag is the blurring of the television image, or "stickiness," when the fluoroscopic tower is moved rapidly. Lag occurs because it takes a certain amount of time for the image to build up and decay on the vidicon target.

Plumbicon and Image-Orthicon Cameras

A plumbicon camera is simply a vidicon camera with a lead monoxide photoconductor for its target. Plumbicon tubes have two advantages over other vidicon tubes: contrast is not diminished and lag is considerably reduced. Plumbicon camera tubes do have more mottle than other vidicon tubes. The patient will receive less exposure with a plumbicon camera tube.

Image-orthicon cameras are much larger than vidicon and plumbicon tubes. An image-orthicon tube functions as both an image intensifier and a pick-up tube. They are extremely sensitive to light and function well with low levels of illumination. More importantly, the image-orthicon tube has superior resolution and complete freedom from lag.

Image-orthicon tubes have the following serious disadvantages:

1. They are too expensive for most radiology departments.
2. Their large size makes them cumbersome to operate.
3. They are extremely sensitive to temperature changes.
4. They require a long warm-up time (up to 20 min.).

Charge-Coupled Device (CCD)

Conventional video camera tubes have been replaced in many units by a solid state component known as a **charge-coupled device**. This device is a semiconductor that has the ability to store charge from light photons striking a photosensitive surface in localized areas and to later transfer this charge to an appropriate display terminal. The advantage provided by solid state technology is a unit that is smaller in size, lower in power consumption, and has a longer life. More importantly, CCDs have a very fast discharge time, which eliminates image lag. This is very useful in high-speed imaging applications such as cardiac catheterization.

Kell Factor

The **Kell factor** is defined as the ratio between the vertical resolution and the number of scan lines in the television system. The Kell factor measures **vertical** resolution. Kell factors are determined experimentally by measuring the maximum number of lines that can be seen with a line pair imaging system. The Kell factor can be computed using the following formula:

$$\text{Kell factor} = \frac{\text{Resolution}}{\text{Number of scan lines}}$$

The Kell factor for a 525-scan-line system is 0.7.

Review Questions

1. Each frame of a television picture consists of _____ scan lines.

2. The input screen of a television camera tube converts the light image from the image intensifier into a(n)
   a. x-ray image.
   b. electronic image.
   c. visible image.
   d. none of the above.

3. The electronic signal which takes the information from the television camera to the monitor is called the _____ signal.

4. In order to ensure the proper eye integration, a frame must be completed every _____ sec.

5. In order to prevent the flicker effect during the viewing of the television image, a technique called _____ is used.

6. The target assembly of the television camera tube consists of _____, _____, and _____.

7. The most important component part of the television monitor is
   a. cathode ray tube.
   b. television camera tube.
   c. electromagnetic coils.
   d. coupling device.

8. One television frame is equivalent to
   a. one television field.
   b. two television fields.
   c. 262.5 lines.
   d. 17 msec.

9. Fluoroscopic television systems operate at a frame rate of _____ frames/sec.

10. Horizontal television resolution is limited principally by the _____.

11. On television systems with automatic exposure control (ABS), the brightness of the image varies directly as mA and as the fifth power of kVp. Thus, as the kVp would vary from 80 to 88 kVp, a 10% change, there could be a _____% change in brightness.

■ Principles of Fluoroscopic Image Intensification and Television Systems: Workbook and Laboratory Manual

12. The weakest link in the televised image-intensified chain is the resolution of the
    a. image intensifier.
    b. coupling device.
    c. cine radiographic camera.
    d. television system.

13. The normal viewing distance for binocular vision is _____ in.

14. The average number of horizontal scan lines on the television monitor is _____ scan lines.

15. Which of the following systems provides the least patient exposure?
    a. image-orthicon tube
    b. plumbicon tube
    c. vidicon tube
    d. mirror optical system

Answers to the review questions are on page 178. If you answered 12 or more items correctly, go to the next chapter. If you answered fewer than 12 items correctly, reread the chapter and retake the review questions.

46

© GR/St. Lucie Press

Chapter 4

Recording the Television Image

Objectives

Upon completion of Chapter 4, the reader will be able to:

1. Discuss the basic principles of magnetic recorders.
2. Describe the material that is used in magnetic tape.
3. Recall the characteristics of video tape recorders.
4. Use video tape recorders and video disc recorders.
5. List the three important factors that influence patient exposure when cinefluororadiography is employed.
6. Explain synchronization, framing frequency, and the f/ number of the cine camera.
7. Compare and contrast the framing frequency and patient exposure.
8. Calculate the patient skin dose when operating the cine camera.
9. Operate the spot-film camera system.
10. List the advantages of the spot-film camera for serial angiography.
11. Operate the film/screen spot-film device.
12. Recall the factors that affect the film/screen spot-film device.

© GR/St. Lucie Press

> 13. Explain how contrast, sharpness, and mottle affect the recorded image.
> 14. Recall the equipment requirements for the image intensifier/television system.

Magnetic Recorders

In the early days of imaging, one of the less desirable aspects of television display was the lack of a means of obtaining a permanent record. The commercial television industry has been storing programs on tape recorders for many years. When magnetic recorders were first developed, they were extremely expensive—too expensive for the radiology department. Recently, less expensive models have been developed. Video tape and video disc magnetic recorders are commonly used to store fluoroscopic images.

Physical Principles

The physical principles of magnetic recorders are the same for video tape and disc recorders. The video tape recorder operates much the same way as does an audio tape recorder. The video signal is directed through a coil of wire wound around a metal core (Figure 4.1).

There is a very small gap in this core, and electric current flowing through the coils of wire creates a magnetic field across this gap. If magnetic material is placed in contact with this gap, it will take on some of the magnetic characteristics and will be transformed into a weak but, nevertheless, permanent magnet. If the electric signal flowing into the coil of wire, or the **recording head**, is varied continuously and if the magnetic material is moved continuously, a permanent record of the

Chapter 4 ■ Recording the Television Image

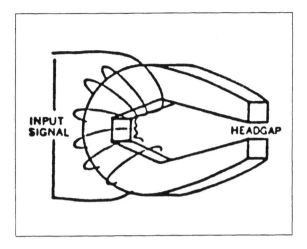

Figure 4.1: Magnetic head.

electrical signal will be realized. In the playback mode of operation, if the same magnetized material is passed across the gap in the recording head, the magnetic field in the material will cause an electric current to be generated in the coil of wire which can be read out, amplified, and used to create the original video signal.

Recording Head

A representative recording head is shown in Figure 4.2. The most significant single characteristic of a recording head is the gap width. This will directly influence the degree of detail or resolution that is impressed on the magnetic tape. In most television tape recorders, the gap width is 0.001 mm.

Magnetic Tape

The magnetic tape consists of a plastic base, such as acetate or polyester, on the surface of which fine particles of magnetic material are dispersed. The magnetic particles contact the recording head at the gap and complete the magnetic path in the recording head core (Fig-

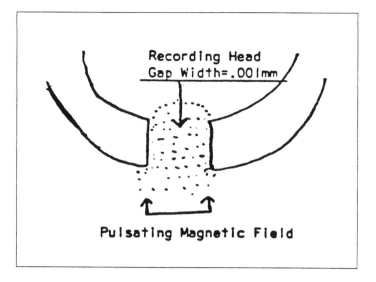

Figure 4.2: Recording head gap width.

ure 4.2). The individual particle size of the magnetic material, which is iron oxide, will influence resolution.

The combination of the recording head gap width and the iron oxide particles will determine what will be in the recording system. Having one with a small tape gap, 0.001 mm, and using small iron particles will record the smallest possible wavelength or bandwidth.

To record a bandwidth of several million cycles per second, the tape must move at very high velocity. This is accomplished by moving both the tape and the writing heads. The tape moves diagonally past paired writing heads mounted on either side of a rapidly revolving drum. The tape moves in one direction at a speed of 10 in./sec., and the writing heads move in the opposite direction at 1,000 in./sec. Each writing head records one video frame as it passes diagonally across the tape. The signal is impressed on separate tracks. The tape moves fast enough to separate the tracks of the two heads. Video tracks are separated by a narrow guard band. A reel tape (3,000 ft) plays approximately one hour.

Video Tape Recorders

Video tape recorders for medical x-ray systems should have several characteristics beyond those of home video recorders. First, they must be capable of remote control operation between stand-by and record. When installed, the video tape recorder can record automatically as the operator depresses the fluoroscopic control (dead man switch). Following or during an examination, a study can be re-examined without exposing the patient to x-rays. Second, the medical image is very noisy. For this reason, a medical-quality tape should be used. Some video tape recorders will allow slow motion or field-by-field observation of the image. When used with fast time constant cameras, the video tape recorder can monitor an injection sequence also recorded by a cineradiographic camera. The video tape can be reviewed immediately to determine whether the injection was adequate or whether a repeat study in another projection is required.

Video Disc Recorders

Video disc recorders are used to record either single fields, single frames, or a short sequence. Some video disc recorders have removable discs so that a sequence of images can be recorded and removed. One application of the video disc recorder is called "sticky" fluoroscopy. The machine records the last full frame of information during a fluoroscopic sequence and displays that frame when the fluoroscopic switch is released. During the procedure, the radiologist presses the foot switch, and real-time information is displayed. When he/she releases the foot switch, the last image freezes and remains on the screen when the x-rays are off. During an examination, the radiologist can momentarily remove his/her foot from the switch and then depress it to record a single frame of information. During an upper gastrointestinal examination, an object of interest may be seen on the screen. The radiologist momentarily removes his/her foot, presses the switch down again, and then, when the x-rays are off, he/she can manually go back to the disc player and display that field or frame for closer scrutiny. At the end of the fluoroscopic sequence, the recorded information can be examined one image at a time.

It is possible to use recorded information on the disc or a specially recorded synchronizing track to lock the image of the television camera to the stored image on the disc. In this way, a scout image can be recorded and subtracted from real-time images of the television camera obtained during the injection. A video tape recorder can then record the different images, which will have the same appearance as a sequence of subtracted films. When disc recorders are used with mobile C-arm assemblies, one image can be recorded with the image intensifier vertical, and the second image can be recorded and displayed with the assembly horizontal to produce image pairs, as is the case for stereotaxic views. A biplane system can also be made to time-share one generator by using a disc recorder to store the image of the non-energized plane.

New developments in electronic memory circuits for computers have led to digital image storage devices. Such devices can record one or two frames of information and take image differences or enhance the edges of displayed objects and, in general, perform many of the functions of the disc recorder. While limited to recording only a few frames, memory circuits have no moving parts and potentially can be produced at low cost.

In summary,

1. Video disc recorders provide a method of lowering the dose to the patient when operating fluoroscopy (i.e., an abdominal fluoroscopic study resulting in 10 R skin entrance dose may be reduced by 95% to 500 mR if a video disc is used).
2. Video disc framing rates vary from a minimum of 1 image/sec. to a maximum of 30 frames/sec.

Cinefluororadiography

The image intensification system provides a bright image for various recording systems. Spot-film cameras and cine cameras are used to record the image from the output phosphor of the image intensifier, while video recordings are obtained from the output of the television camera tube.

Cine Camera

Cine cameras use either 16mm or 35mm film sizes. In the United States, 98% of all cine is done on 35mm film, and 95% of all cine studies involve the heart. Therefore, the major emphasis here will be on 35mm cardiac cinefluororadiography.

More information can be recorded on the 35mm frame since it has four times the area of a 16mm frame. This increased filming area produces images with higher resolution than the 16mm film. Both high-resolution images and the ability to project these images before a large audience can be achieved by an initial recording of the image on 35mm film and then by transferring it onto 16mm fine-grained copy film for projection.

Patient exposure in cinefluororadiography is influenced by three factors:

1. Synchronization.
2. Framing frequency.
3. f/number of the optical system of the camera lens.

The timing and intensity of the x-ray exposure are controlled during cinefluororadiography by two electrical signals that originate from within the cine system. One signal coordinates the x-ray exposure with the open time of the camera shutter (referred to as synchronization), and the other maintains a constant level of intensifier illumination by varying the exposure factors for areas of different thickness or density.

1. **Synchronization.** In all modern cinefluororadiographic systems, the x-ray output is intermittent, and the exposure is synchronized with the open time of the camera shutter. Synchronization is controlled by an electrical signal from commutators and brushes of the camera motor. After the motor opens the shutter and advances the film, it signals the generator to make an exposure. To accomplish synchronization and the high framing rates that are used today (150 frames/sec.), cine cameras must be operated in conjunction with three-phase, twelve-pulse, constant potential generators. Modern cine cameras switch the generator on only when their shutters are open. This requires extremely rapid switching of the x-ray beam on and off during a filming series. Such rapid switching causes the x-rays to occur in pulses controlled by either the constant potential generator or grid-controlled x-ray tubes. The wave from the generator must be constant so that each frame of the cine film is exposed with the same density. Since the cine camera records its information from the output screen of the image intensifier, its resolution is not as good as that obtained by direct spot-film radiography. This loss in image resolution is compensated for, in cine angiography, by the fact that the image quality of cine film is improved by the integration power of the human eye when the projected cine film is viewed at fast film rates. Field sizes and magnification factors can be controlled in cinefluorography by changing the ratio of the focal length of the cine camera lens.

2. **Framing frequency.** The framing frequency, or the number of frames/sec., is usually 60 divided or multiplied by a whole number (i.e., 7.5, 15, 30, 60, 120). The combination of the framing frequency and shutter opening determines the amount of time available for both the exposure and pull-down. For example, with a 180° shutter opening and 60 frames/sec., the

time available for both the exposure and pull-down is $1/120$ sec. At slower framing frequencies, both are longer. With a smaller shutter opening, the available exposure time is shorter than the pull-down time.

3. **f/number of the optical system.** The cine optical system is designed to be as fast as reasonable cost and modern technology permit. The speed of the lens is determined by its ability to concentrate light at the image plane. Concentration refers to light intensity per unit area and depends on both the total quantity of available light and the area over which it is distributed. The speed of the lens is indicated by an "f" number, usually written as f/4 or f/8. The lower f/number is determined by dividing the focal length of a lens by its diameter. f/numbers are expressed in the following standard series: 0.70, 1.0, 1.4, 2.0, 2.8, 4.0, 5.6, 8.0, 11, 16, and so forth. Each lowered number "f" stop allows twice as much light to reach the image plane as the next higher f/number in the series. An f/2.8 lens, then, is twice as fast as an f/4.0 lens and four times as fast as an f/5.6 lens.

Framing and Patient Exposure

The term framing refers to the use of the available film area. Regarding 35mm cine film, the Inter-Society Commission for Heart Disease Resources has classified various degrees of cine framing.

1. **Underframing.** The maximum size of the fluoroscopic image is smaller than the smallest dimension of the frame. Underframing should be avoided due to faulty optical system.

2. **Exact framing.** The diameter of the intensifier image at the output phosphor and the smallest dimension of the cine frame (18mm) are the same. No part of the image is lost, but only 58% of the cine frame is used.

3. **Overframing**. The diameter of the circular image from the optical system is larger than the shortest dimension of the film. Therefore, part of the image is lost.

4. **Total overframing**. The diameter of the circular image from the optical system is equal to the diagonal measurement of the rectangular aperture (30mm). All of the film is used, but 39% of the image is wasted.

The x-ray beam must be restricted to match the framing method. If the x-ray beam is not correspondingly restricted, areas of the patient are exposed, but the image is never recorded. All fluoroscopic units have rectangular field collimators. The cine frame is rectangular (24mm × 18mm), the image intensifier is round, and the x-ray field is square or rectangular. With this arrangement of shapes, a portion of either the x-ray field or the image intensifier is wasted with all framing methods except **total overframing**. With other framing methods some portion of the recorded image is lost. By using **exact framing**, none of the image is wasted, but the x-ray field is 1.3 times as large as the image intensifier. The patient exposure is comparably great in terms of area.

On the other hand, **total overframing** increases the patient exposure. The exposed patient area is 2.1 times greater than the recorded area. To decrease patient exposure, one solution would be to restrict the x-ray beam to the recorded area and not the image intensifier.

The Inter-Society Commission for Heart Disease Resources recommends a minimum exposure of 20 μR/frame (μR/frame = microroentgen/frame, a microroentgen being 1 one-millionth of a roentgen and, thus, 1 one-thousandth of a milliroentgen) for cinefluorography, measured at the input of the image intensifier. Using this figure, it is possible to calculate the patient's skin exposure as follows:

Chapter 4 ▪ Recording the Television Image

> 1. Assuming that only 1% of the initial beam actually reaches the image intensifier due to patient and grid absorption and the inverse square law, the patient will receive a skin exposure that is 100 times as great as the exposure measured at the image intensifier.
>
> 2. 100×20 µR/frame = 2,000 µR/frame
>
> 3. Convert µR/frame to milliroentgen/frame: 2,000 µR/frame $\times$ 1 mR/1,000 µR = 2 mR/frame
>
> 4. Convert 2 mR/frame to patient skin exposure per minute (mR/min.) when the framing frequency is, for example, 30 frames/sec.: 2 mR/frame $\times$ 30 frame/sec. $\times$ 60 sec./min. = 3,600 mR/min.
>
> 5. Convert mR/min. to R/min.: 3,600 mR/min. $\times$ 1 R/1,000 mR = 3.6 R/min.

Quality Assurance

The quality assurance program for cinefluororadiography equipment shall be as follows:

1. Perform inspection at least once each year.
2. Perform inspection immediately following alterations or replacements of major components.
3. Determine the useful x-ray beam exposure rate.

Spot-Film Camera System

Spot-film cameras are almost identical to cine cameras but require a lens with a longer focal length to cover the larger film formats. Spot-film cameras use either 70, 90, 100, or 105mm roll or cut film sizes.

© GR/St. Lucie Press

Spot-film cameras are used in two different fluoroscopic examinations. Initially, their use was limited to gastrointestinal fluoroscopy because of the lower resolution and contrast of the silver-activated zinc cadmium sulfide phosphors in the image intensification tube. Gastrointestinal studies did not require a high-resolution imaging system. After cesium iodide phosphors were introduced in the image intensification tube, spot-film cameras have been used for serial filming in various kinds of angiography examinations. This provides a great savings in film cost, but the image detail with spot-film cameras is not as good as with direct serial radiography.

The principal advantage of spot-film cameras over direct radiographic filming methods is a substantial reduction in patient exposure. More specifically, the advantages of spot-film cameras for serial angiography are as follows:

1. Reduced procedure time.
2. Increased ease in the performance of these exams.
3. Constant monitoring of the images becomes possible during the performance of the examination.
4. Shorter exposure times.
5. Reduced cost in film and processing.

Film/Screen Spot-Film Device

Most image-intensified fluoroscopic systems employ a film/screen spot-film device for recording the image. To expose a spot film, the operator adjusts the field size to accommodate the anatomic part and then moves the film cassette in place by turning the power assist handle on the fluoroscopic tower or an appropriate switch on the control generator. The film cassette will move from a lead-shielded storage compartment into the fluoroscopic field. The fluoroscopic x-ray tube current is automatically adjusted and increased from approximately 3.0 mA to a more conventional radiographic level of 100 up to 1,000 mA of tube current. The exposure time is adjusted by an ion chamber type of phototimer.

Factors Affecting Film/Screen Spot-Film Image Quality

Detail perception for a radiographic or fluoroscopic spot film depends on the same technical factors, with the exception of brightness, as it does in fluoroscopy (i.e., contrast, sharpness, and mottle).

1. **Contrast.** Radiographic or fluoroscopic contrast is the difference in the density between the object of interest and its surroundings. As in fluoroscopy, it can be divided into **display contrast** and **subject contrast.** More contrast can be obtained using a film/screen combination than using 100mm or 105mm spot-film cameras. The grid employed during fluoroscopy also is employed frequently in film/screen spot filming, although in certain high-contrast examinations, such as full column barium enemas, films of diagnostic quality can be obtained for small field sizes (i.e., four-on-one spot) without employing a grid. Shorter exposure times and reduced patient motion result. The decrease in patient motion associated with shorter exposure time generally more than offsets the loss in contrast. In addition, for certain low-contrast examinations such as gallbladder, improved spot films can be obtained for small field sizes without a grid by employing lower kVp techniques. For larger field sizes, it has been suggested that a second linear grid with its strips positioned orthogonal to those of the fluoroscopic grid be incorporated during spot filming. Such grid arrangements have been introduced recently by certain x-ray equipment manufacturers and allow the selection of a single linear grid for smaller patients and crossed grids for larger patients. The use of crossed grids results in substantial contrast improvement on larger patients. On smaller patients, the improvement is less

noticeable and is not usually sufficient to offset the increase in radiation exposure that results when the second grid is employed.

2. **Sharpness**. The sharpness of a film/screen spot film depends on image receptor sharpness, focal spot size, geometry (or magnification), and patient motion.

3. **Noise**. The mottle in a radiographic or fluoroscopic image is the fluctuation in film density from one area to another. Film granularity and quantum mottle both contribute to noise. More importantly, the closer one views the film/screen spot-film image, the greater is the amount of quantum noise perceived.

Equipment Requirements

The fluoroscopic unit selected by a radiologist will be influenced mainly by the type and imaging requirements of the examinations to be performed. Examinations in which the table can be simple and fixed in the horizontal position are arthrograms, enteroclysis, retained stone removal, and checking of the position of biopsy and diagnostic devices and tubes.

A motor-driven fluoroscopic table that can tilt 90° from the horizontal is generally adequate for conventional upper gastrointestinal and colon examinations, ERCP (endoscopic retrograde cholangiopancreatography), T-tube cholangiography, gallbladder spot films, and voiding cystourography. A table that can tilt 90° in one direction and 75° or 90° in the other is desirable for myelography, air contrast gastrointestinal studies, and bronchography.

The capability for filming and fluoroscopically imaging fine detail is required for most angiographic procedures, air contrast gastrointestinal examinations, arthrography, sialography, and ERCP. The capability of imaging fine detail is also desirable in cardiac and lung fluoroscopy. Less detail is acceptable in some high-contrast studies. These include the full column barium enema and gastrointestinal studies, myelography, cholecystography, voiding cystography, and fluoroscopic examinations to monitor tube placement and diaphragm movement.

Less detailed examinations can be accommodated by either a 6-in. or 9-in. single-field image intensifier, a 1.0-mm focal spot with a 12° target x-ray tube, and a conventional spot-film device using fast or moderately fast rare-earth screens. Recently available large field (12, 14, and 16 in.) image intensifiers can also be employed for such examinations. They would eliminate the need for overhead films, thereby increasing patient throughput and offsetting, to some extent, their greater cost. High-speed anode rotation is a desirable feature, and in gastrointestinal and ERCP examinations, where patient motion can be a problem, it is essential. The image intensifier can be viewed with either a television or mirror system, and spot filming can be accomplished with a 100mm or 105mm camera.

For fine detail examinations, it is advisable to have a dual- or, preferably, triple-field image intensifier coupled with a 0.3mm focal spot. The finest detail will be realized when the image intensifier is operated in the 4.5-in. magnification mode with 2× geometrical magnification in the optical system. If the coupled image intensifier is viewed with a television system, 875 scan lines is preferable.

High-quality radiographic film can be obtained by employing a relatively sharp, moderate speed, rare-earth film screen combination with a 1.25× geometrical magnification of the optical system and a 0.6mm focal spot or by employing a relatively fast rare-earth film screen combination with 2× magnification and a 0.3mm focal spot. High-quality fluorographic spot films can be obtained with a 100mm or 105mm camera and the image intensifier in the 4.5-in. magnification mode. If the patient area to be recorded is sufficiently small and motion is not a problem, fluorographic detail can be further increased by employing a 0.3mm focal spot and greater than $2\times$ geometrical magnification. High-speed anode rotation should be employed in both cases to reduce exposure time and patient motion.

Review Questions

1. What is the commonly used video disc frame rate?
   a. 1 frame/sec.
   b. 5 frames/sec.
   c. 15 frames/sec.
   d. 30 frames/sec.

2. When using a spot-film camera, the film size that results in the greatest dose to the patient is
   a. 35mm.
   b. 70mm.
   c. 90mm.
   d. 105mm.

3. The purpose of synchronization of the cine camera is _____ _____.

4. In most magnetic tape recorders, the gap width is on the order of _____mm.

5. The recording head of the video tape receives a changing electric signal that is transformed into a changing _____.

6. With cineradiographic equipment, the exposure rates that patients are subjected to shall be determined by a qualified individual _____ _____.

7. When using the vidicon television tube, a problem that occurs is the blurring or "lag" of the image as the camera is moved during the procedure. This lag or blurring occurs because _____.

8. During a cine exam in which a frame rate of 30 frames/sec. is used, what is the approximate skin exposure?

9. Patient exposure, when using cineradiography, is influenced by_____ _____, _____, and _____.

10. Total overframing of the cine recording device will
    a. produce a brighter image.
    b. increase resolution.
    c. increase patient exposure.
    d. all of the above.

Answers to the review questions are on page 178. If you answered 7 or more items correctly, go to the next chapter. If you answered fewer than 7 items correctly, reread the chapter and retake the review questions.

Chapter 5

Computerized Fluoroscopic Image Intensification

Objectives

Upon completion of Chapter 5, the reader will be able to:

1. Describe computerized image intensification mode.
2. Discuss mask mode image intensification.
3. Identify the elements of mask mode intensification.
4. Explain time interval difference mode.
5. Assess K-edge image intensification.
6. Describe hybrid versus unmixed digital techniques.
7. Establish the x-ray exposure rate for computerized image intensification.

Computerized Fluoroscopy

The advantages of time-subtraction angiography, in which a preinjection film is subtracted from postinjection films, are well known. However, the superimposition of several pairs of films is tedious and impractical for generating displays with frame rates approaching those used in image intensification. More importantly, once the information of interest has been isolated, there is no convenient means of increasing the image contrast by large factors.

Through digital electronic technology, analogous to that used in computerized tomography, several time and energy subtraction algorithms have been developed. The equipment used for this purpose consists of an image intensifier, a digital image processor, a control computer, and a means for storing a sequence of subtraction images such as a video tape or disc recording. The computer is used to preset the digital circuitry, which actually performs the chosen algorithm and generally does not operate on image information except in non-realtime postprocessing of information stored on the tape or disc.

Mask Mode Image Intensification

This procedure is analogous to film subtraction angiography but may differ in several important ways. The elements of this mode include the following:

1. Logarithmic processing of the video information.

2. Integration of preinjection video images over times typical of 0.5 sec.

3. Use of a heavily filtered x-ray beam.

4. Subtraction of postinjection information at rates up to 60 images/sec.

Logarithmic processing of the data prior to subtraction is necessary to ensure that in the subtracted images, a given amount of iodine used for angiography will produce the same residual signal independent of the local

Chapter 5 ▪ Computerized Fluoroscopic Image Intensification

image brightness in the subtracted images. Integration of preinjection video images ensures that the quantum, statistical, and electrical noise in the preinjected mask are negligible. An alternative approach to provide a mask of negligible noise is to employ a high tube current and a specialized low-noise video camera. The latter approach yields a sharper mask in the presence of motion.

There are advantages and disadvantages to the sharp mask, which depend on the details of the application. When imaging coronary arteries following intravenous injection, subtraction of phase-related sharp masks may be necessary to minimize unsubtracted background. However, for continuous study of cardiac chamber performance and ventricular wall motion, a time-integrated mask, though not sharp, may be adequate. Sharp masks have permitted subtraction images to be digitally amplified by factors of 10 or more relative to the unprocessed images. Therefore, adequate visualization of left ventricular wall motion can be achieved with contrast volumes as small as 2 ml.

Time Interval Difference (TID) Mode

It is possible to subtract transmission information associated with more closely spaced time intervals of $1/_{15}$ sec. instead of using a preinjection mask. These images display the change in x-ray transmission or, in most applications, the change in iodine path length. TID procedures may be obtained in real time during the first pass of iodine bolus or by reprocessing the mask mode from video disc or tape. The TID mode is insensitive to respiratory motion. Therefore, it may be used in extracting information from procedures in which significant patient motion has occurred. The TID display is much less dependent on patient cooperation. Moreover, it can often be used to salvage examinations that otherwise may have been unsuccessful due to motion artifacts.

© GR/St. Lucie Press

K-Edge Image Intensification

The TID mode displays changes in iodine content rather than the instantaneous iodine concentration which requires a dynamic state. K-edge image intensification is another method to display dynamic iodine images without respiratory motion. K-edge intensification relies on the abrupt increase in iodine attenuation coefficient at the 33-keV K-edge. A partially monoenergetic x-ray beam is formed by filtration with cerium, which forms an x-ray beam with average energies above the iodine K-edge. Since bone and soft tissue attenuation coefficients undergo a much smaller change, as the beam energy is moved from below the K-edge to above, a difference image using the cerium- and iodine-filtered beams will suppress these substances and isolate the iodine signal. This signal can be greatly amplified.

Presently, K-edge image intensification mode is limited to x-ray tube power requirements. Cine-pulsed operation at 60 pulses/sec. at 1,000 mA at 50 kVp will not provide enough input exposure for an adult human heart due to the attenuation of iodine and cerium filters.

Combination vs. Unmixed Digital Techniques

Mask mode image intensification and radiography may be accomplished by two separate techniques. Pure digital subtraction, in which preinjection images and postinjection images are identically processed, provides the most precise cancellation of anatomy and flexibility in terms of processing options. However, in other situations, a combination of analog and digital techniques may be used to permit inexpensive implementation of the simplest computerized image-intensified algorithms with high resolution.

Chapter 5 ■ Computerized Fluoroscopic Image Intensification

In this situation, a low-resolution preinjection mask is stored digitally and reconverted to analog form to permit subtraction with postinjection undigitized video. The postinjection video channel should be of high resolution in order to display the high spatial frequency components of the injected iodine information. If the anatomical background does not contain significant high-contrast signals at high spatial frequencies, the low-resolution digitally stored preinjected mask will cancel the anatomy and permit a factor of 10 amplification of injected iodine signals. In this manner, high-resolution iodine information may be obtained without large amounts of memory or high digitization rates.

Encounter with the combination technique has established that good images may be obtained of the heart, lungs, and kidneys. However, in the head, the presence of high spatial frequency information from the bone leads to unsubtracted anatomical backgrounds. The combination subtraction procedure done with a 525-scan-line television system provides better detail and could be extended easily to higher resolution simply by replacing the video system with one of higher resolution.

X-ray Exposure with Computerized Image Intensification

X-ray exposures required for the imaging and subtraction methods may be comparable to those used in computerized tomography. The required exposure increases as spatial resolution requirements are increased and as the contrast of the subject to be imaged is decreased. Therefore, for intravenous angiography, x-ray exposure is related to (1) the amount of contrast injected, (2) the spatial resolution of the subtracted computer hardware, and (3) patient thickness and x-ray beam energy.

© GR/St. Lucie Press

The typical exposure rate for the human left heart study is on the order of 200 milliRoentgen/sec. The duration of exposure may vary from a few seconds, if only the left ventricle is studied, to 10 or 15 seconds, if the entire bolus of contrast is to be followed from the right heart to the aorta.

In typical exposures for examinations other than the heart (e.g., the carotid arteries or kidneys), irradiating the patient is reduced by delaying the exposure until the time of arrival of the contrast in the area of interest. In order to minimize the possibility of motion artifacts, the patient can be instructed to suspend breathing shortly after injection rather than before. The mask image is taken during passage of the bolus of contrast to the site of interest.

The Future of Computerized Image Intensification

The range of applications for computerized image intensification is abundant. The efficacy of this modality as compared to conventional techniques and tomography suggests areas of usefulness.

All x-ray transmission examinations are characterized by their contrast resolution, spatial resolution, and characteristic imaging times. Conventional film radiography offers the highest spatial resolution and has reasonably good temporal properties but has poor contrast resolution. Cinefluororadiography has good spatial resolution and excellent imaging rates, but poor contrast resolution. Computed tomography offers excellent contrast resolution, moderate spatial resolution, and poor temporal properties on the order of one second or more.

Computerized image intensification plays an important role in clinical examinations requiring excellent contrast resolution, moderate spatial resolution similar to television resolution, and excellent transitory resolution on the order of 60 images/sec. Computerized image intensification is sustaining revolutionary changes. The potential use of computerized image intensification and its distinct imaging algorithms is just beginning. Since many of these algorithms, including those which appear to be most useful, only require processing of conventional image-intensified images, the apparatus needed for computerization may become readily available as an accessory item to upgrade an existing fluoroscopic image-intensified system.

■ Principles of Fluoroscopic Image Intensification and Television Systems: Workbook and Laboratory Manual

Review Questions

1. Logarithmic processing of the data prior to subtraction is necessary to ensure that
   a. a given amount of contrast is used.
   b. the contrast will produce the same residual signal in the subtracted image.
   c. the noise is negligible.
   d. it produces quantum noise.

2. Subtraction of phase-related sharp masks is necessary to
   a. maximize unsubtracted background.
   b. digitally amplify by a factor of 5.
   c. minimize the unsubtracted background.
   d. digitally amplify by a factor of 10.

3. TID mode is insensitive to
   a. motion artifacts.
   b. cardiac activity.
   c. respiratory motion.
   d. all of the above.

4. K-edge image intensification mode is limited to
   a. x-ray tube power requirements.
   b. tissue density.
   c. anatomic part thickness.
   d. atomic number differences.

5. The typical x-ray exposure rate for the left heart study is
   a. 0.2 R.
   b. 200 R.
   c. 2000 mR.
   d. none of the above.

Answers to the review questions are on page 178. If you answered 3 or more items correctly, go to the next chapter. If you answered fewer than 3 items correctly, reread the chapter and retake the review questions.

© GR/St. Lucie Press

Chapter 6

Fluoroscopic Image Production

Objectives

Upon completion of Chapter 6, the reader will be able to:

1. Recall the characteristics of electromagnetic radiation.
2. Define thermionic emission.
3. Describe the production of Bremsstrahlung radiation.
4. Describe the production of characteristic radiation.
5. Explain how x-rays interact with matter.
6. Identify the photoelectric effect.
7. List the characteristics of Compton scatter.

Electromagnetic Radiation

The electromagnetic spectrum has been thoroughly surveyed and sufficient proof established that these are all forms of the same type of energy. Figure 6.1 is a diagram of the electromagnetic spectrum. It encompasses a wide range of energy from cosmic, gamma, and x-rays at the short-wavelength region up to infrared, microwave, and electrical waves in the long-wavelength region.

© GR/St. Lucie Press

■ Principles of Fluoroscopic Image Intensification and Television Systems: Workbook and Laboratory Manual

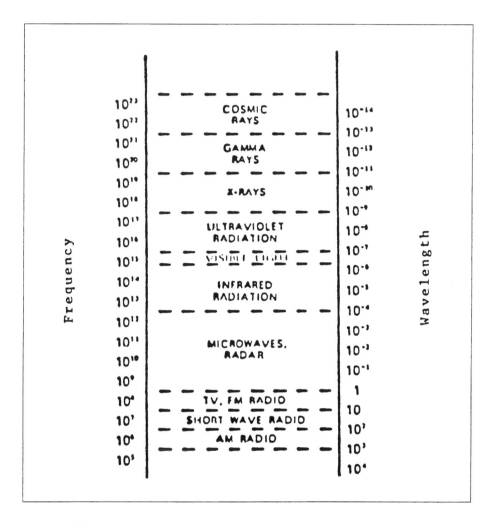

Figure 6.1: Relationship between energy and wavelength.

Characteristics

Electromagnetic energies that are present in space as bundles of electrical and magnetic fields are arranged in nature in an orderly fashion according to the wavelength of their energies. When we speak of long and short wavelength in the portion of the x-ray spectrum in which medical x-rays are found, we are limiting our discussion to a range from approximately 0.1 A to 0.5 A. When this energy is transported through space, it is referred to as **electromagnetic radiation** and travels in the form of waves at the speed of light, about 186,000 mi./sec.

The sinewave oscillation can be characterized by

1. **Amplitude**. The height of the wave from crest to average or from valley bottom to average.
2. **Wavelength**. The distance from one crest to another or the distance between two corresponding points on the wave.
3. **Frequency**. The number of crests or valleys passing by a specific point in a given unit of time.
4. **Velocity**. Electromagnetic radiation always travels at the same velocity in a vacuum. This velocity is 186,000 mi./sec. (3×10^8 mi./sec.), which is usually referred to as the velocity of light and given the symbol $\underline{C}$.

   Therefore, we can express the relationship between velocity, wavelength, and frequency as $\underline{C} = \lambda \vartheta$.

$$\underline{C} = \text{velocity of light}$$
$$\lambda = \text{wavelength}$$
$$\vartheta = \text{frequency}$$

The smallest particle of any type of electromagnetic radiation is called a **photon** or a **quantum** of energy that is thought of as a small bundle of energy having no mass and no charge. The energy of the photon emitted from a radiation source is directly proportional to the frequency *or* inversely proportional to the wavelength of the radiation. For example, high energies have short wavelength and long (high) frequencies, and low energies have long wavelengths and short (low) frequencies.

There is considerable overlap in the wavelengths of the various members of the electromagnetic spectrum. The numbers listed in Figure 6.1 are rough guides. It is again stressed that the great differences in properties of these different types of radiation are attributable to their differences in wavelengths (or frequencies).

The wave concept of electromagnetic radiation explains why it may be reflected, refracted, diffracted, and polarized. The unit used to measure the energy of photons is the electron volt (eV). An **electron volt** is the amount of energy that an electron gains as it is accelerated by a potential difference of one volt (i.e., 1 volt of EMF = 1 eV of energy). Because the electron volt is a small unit, x-ray energies are usually measured in terms of the **kiloelectron volt** (keV), which is 1,000 times the electron volt. The following equation shows the relationship between energy and wavelength for various photon energies:

$$E = \frac{12.4}{\lambda}$$

E = energy (in keV)

λ = wavelength (in Angstroms)

12.4 = Velocity of light ($\underline{C}$) times Plank's Constant

Production of X-radiation

X-rays are produced when rapidly moving electrons interact with the nucleus of the atoms of a target (anode) of the x-ray tube (see Figure 6.2), which when heated to incandescence causes electrons to "boil off" in a process known as **thermionic emission**. The potential difference (voltage) between the terminals of the cathode (–) and the anode (+) pulls the "released electrons" from the vicinity of the filament across the tube to strike the anode. This is also referred to as the **tube current** and is measured in milliamperes (mA). X-ray beam intensity is influenced by both tube current (mA) and the applied voltage (kVp). The milliampere setting on the x-ray generator (control panel) determines the heat of the filament (filament current) and, therefore, the number of released electrons available for interaction with the target. The range of the applied voltage (kVp) determines the wavelength and, therefore, the energy of the x-ray photons.

Chapter 6 ■ Fluoroscopic Image Production

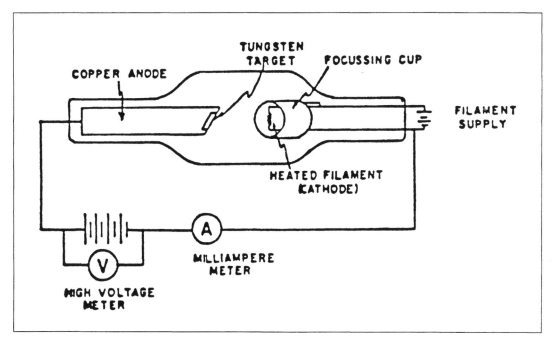

Figure 6.2: Typical anode-cathode x-ray tube.

Interaction of Electron Beam with X-ray Tube Target

When electrons interact with the atoms of the target (anode) of the x-ray tube, the following occurs:

1. **Production of Bremsstrahlung radiation.** This process involves electrons that grazingly pass by the heavy nuclei of the metallic atoms in the target material. The attraction between the electrons (negatively charged) and the nuclei (positively charged) causes the electrons to be deflected and decelerated from their original path and lose some of their energies. Since energy cannot be destroyed, the energies lost by the electrons are transformed and emitted as x-ray photons (Figure 6.3). This radiation is known as a general radiation, the continuous spectrum, white radiation, or **Bremsstrahlung radiation.** As deceleration varies, so does the intensity of the resultant x-ray energy. In the 80-kVp to 100-kVp range, using a tungsten target, these Bremsstrahlung rays constitute about 90% of the radiation emitted

as x-rays. Brems radiation produces polyenergetic radiation. Increasing the voltage generates an increased number of x-rays with shorter wavelengths and, therefore, a more energetic or penetrating beam.

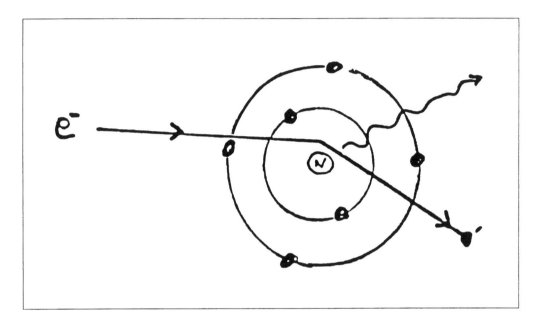

Figure 6.3: Bremsstrahlung radiation.

2. **Characteristic radiation.** Characteristic radiation occurs as electrons emitted from the hot filament collide with the atoms of the target and displace structural electrons from any inner shell of the target atom. Approximately 10% of the x-radiation emitted at 80 kVp to 100 kVp is characteristic radiation. The incoming electron must be of sufficient energy to dislodge any inner shell electron by overcoming its binding energy. Electrons from other shells move in to fill this lower level vacancy. The x-ray photons emitted by this action have wavelengths equal to the difference in energy between the various shells involved in the interaction. The excess energy resulting from the electron transition to a k-shell is usually emitted as an x-ray photon (Figure 6.4).

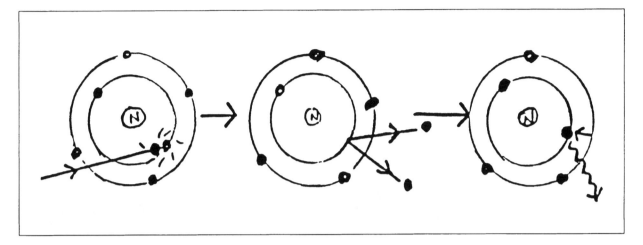

Figure 6.4: Characteristic radiation.

If this interaction occurs in the innermost k-shell, the wavelength of the characteristic radiation is determined by the composition of the target material and the binding power of the k-shell of the atoms in the target. To produce characteristic radiation with a tungsten target, at least 70 kVp is required for k-shell interaction, since the k-shell electron of tungsten is held with 69.53 keV.

X-ray Interaction with Matter

The interaction of x-radiation with matter is significant in fluoroscopy. Every effort must be made to reduce the amount of non-useful ionization of patient tissue by x-ray bombardment. This can be accomplished by the careful use of highly specialized equipment, fluoroscopic accessories, superior fluoroscopic techniques, and optimal radiation protection methods.

The following types of x-ray energies are important to fluoroscopy:

1. Primary x-rays or photons emitted by the x-ray tube.
2. Scattered x-rays or photons produced when primary photons collide with electrons in matter.
3. Remnant radiation or the rays that pass through the patient striking the image detector or fluoroscopic screens.

When x-rays pass through matter, the interactions continue until the primary energy and the energies of the secondary and characteristic radiations are spent. Two x-ray interactions with matter of significant importance, required in the production of a radiographic image, are:

1. **Photoelectric effect**. When an inner shell electron of an atom is struck by an x-ray photon (A), the photon may give off all of its energy. This photon collision causes photoelectric effect (Figure 6.5).

   The electron struck by the x-ray photon is emitted as a photoelectron and is quickly absorbed. The electron ejected as a photoelectron is quickly replaced by another electron from any outer shell (B) or any free electron. The characteristic radiation (thermal energy) emitted is determined by the binding energies of the shells participating in this event.

   The vacancy created in the outer shell by the movement of an electron to fill the inner shell results in an atom with a deficiency of one electron (ionized) (C).

2. **Compton scatter**. When the kilovoltage value is increased, the incoming x-ray photon has increased energy. This photon can strike an electron in an outer shell and be deviated from its original path with a reduction in energy (Figure 6.6).

   This photon will then travel in a different direction but with less energy. The process can be multiplied if the incident photon retains part of its energy and the remaining energy becomes a recoil electron. This interaction is called **Compton effect of scattering**, and many secondary collisions may occur with additional Compton and recoil electrons being generated.

Chapter 6 ■ Fluoroscopic Image Production

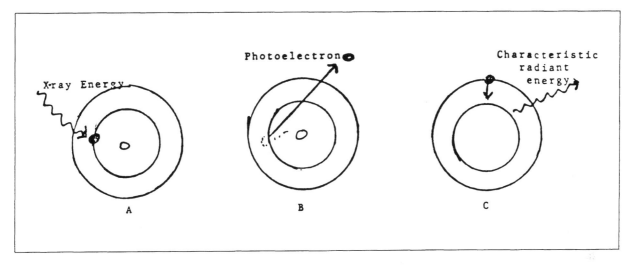

Figure 6.5: Photoelectric effect.

If the incoming photon is of sufficient energy to dislodge the electron, in addition to giving up some of the photon energy, the recoil electron (ejected electron) causes a vacancy in the outer shell, and the atom becomes unstable (ionized).

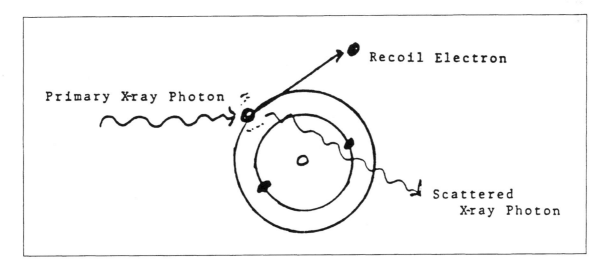

Figure 6.6: Compton scattering.

X-ray photons possess no mass. When the x-ray photon collides with the inner shell electron of an atom, the photon may give off all of its energy, and the collision causes the photoelectric effect (absorption) along with ionization.

The photoelectric effect occurs mainly when low to moderate x-ray energies interact with high atomic absorbers such as bone, barium, and iodine and is a contributing factor to the differential absorption and contrast on the fluoroscopic image. Photoelectric effect will produce a dim image on the fluoroscopic monitor.

Scatter

If the incoming x-ray photon has increased energy resulting from increased kilovoltage applied to the x-ray tube, the x-ray photon, when striking an electron, gives up part of its energy and is deviated from its original path with reduction in energy. Part of the incident x-ray energy is retained, and the remaining energy goes to a recoil electron as kinetic energy. The Compton scattered photons may have other secondary collisions and eject more Compton or recoil electrons until their energy is finally spent.

Photons are scattered in all directions at low energies, with most scattering occurring in a forward direction at high energies. With an increase in kVp, the production of scattered radiation rapidly increases.

An increase in Compton scatter will diminish the quality of the fluoroscopic image. Increased Compton scatter will increase the contrast of the fluoroscopic monitor image by increasing quantum mottle.

Review Questions

1. All radiation coming from the x-ray tube, except the useful beam, is referred to as _____ radiation.

2. Radiant energy that is capable of freeing orbital electrons from the atom is referred to as _____ radiation.

3. The radiolysis of water is the production of free _____.

4. Brems radiation transforms the kinetic energy of the electron into _____ energy.

5. Higher x-ray energies have _____ wavelengths and _____ frequencies.

6. The _____ refers to the height of the wavelength peak.

7. Boiling off a number of electrons from the filament of the x-ray tube is accomplished by selecting the appropriate _____ station.

8. The current going across the x-ray tube gap is called the _____ current.

9. The penetrability of the x-ray energy is determined by the _____.

10. Photoelectric absorption is the interaction between the x-ray energy and the _____ orbital electrons.

11. In the Compton scatter process, the incident photon interacts with a _____ electron.

Answers to chapter review questions are on page 178. If you answered 8 or more items correctly, go to the next chapter. If you answered fewer than 8 items correctly, reread this chapter and retake the review questions.

Chapter 7

Factors Affecting Patient and Operator Exposure

Objectives

Upon completion of Chapter 7, the reader will be able to:

1. List the technical factors that directly influence the exposure rate at the panel or table top.
2. Define tube current and discuss its effect on patient exposure.
3. Describe how kilovoltage peak affects patient exposure.
4. Explain how collimation of the x-ray beam affects patient exposure.
5. Relate how filtration affects the useful x-ray beam.
6. Explain how exposure time affects patient exposure.
7. Recall the allowable exposure rate for image intensification with automatic exposure control.
8. Recall the allowable exposure rate without automatic exposure control.
9. Identify the type of low-absorption table-top material.

© GR/St. Lucie Press

■ Principles of Fluoroscopic Image Intensification and Television Systems: Workbook and Laboratory Manual

The following technical factors **directly** influence the exposure rate at the panel or table top and also influence the patient and operator exposure:

1. **Milliamperage** (mA) tube current is a measure of x-ray tube current of which the intensity of the beam is measured. It is a measure of x-ray **quantity**. It is the product of current of the beam and time during which the electrons strike the target. Doubling the mA will double the patient dose.

   X-ray intensity is directly proportional to the mA (tube current) used. If the mA setting is reduced from 5 mA to 3 mA, the exposure rate is correspondingly reduced by 40% of the initial exposure. The mA (tube current) is typically less than 5 mA as compared to the spot-film cassette tube current, which is greater than 100 mA.

2. **Kilovoltage peak** (kVp) refers to the **quality** of the beam. High kVp technique used for fluoroscopic examinations tends to reduce patient exposure because the improved x-ray beam quality allows the use of a much lower tube current (mA).

   Differential absorption in the patient increases as the kVp is lowered, since there is less penetration of the body part. Therefore, lower kVp levels will result in an increase in the patient dose. The consensus is that while higher kVp slightly increases internal organ dose, it is more than offset by the marked reduction in patient skin dose. Although increased kVp does decrease the patient's skin dose, the higher energy photons that are scattered internally can travel farther prior to their complete interaction with the tissue of the body. This results in an increase in internal organ dose.

   At 120 kVp, the radiation exposure rate at the output phosphor side of the image intensifier will be great. This is caused by the greater penetrating power of the x-ray beam at a high kilovoltage rating.

3. **Collimation** of the x-ray beam must be adjusted so an unexposed border on the input image intensifier

86

© GR/St. Lucie Press

Chapter 7 ■ Factors Affecting Patient and Operator Exposure

phosphor is visible when the image intensifier carriage is positioned 14 in. above the table top and when collimators are fully open. The radiation exposure rate at the input phosphor is independent of x-ray beam size. Therefore, the image will not be brighter with a larger beam size. However, the total volume of the patient that is exposed to radiation will increase, as well as the amount of scattered radiation to the operator.

More importantly, image quality will improve as the size of the x-ray beam is reduced because there is a reduction in the amount of scattered radiation reaching the image intensifier. In other words, using proper collimation will reduce quantum mottle.

When operating the image intensifier, the operator must always restrict the x-ray beam to the size that is practical to the examination. Increasing the size of the exposure field will increase patient exposure.

4. **Filtration** is any material placed in the useful (primary) x-ray beam to absorb less penetrating radiations. At 85 kVp and with a 0.5-mm aluminum filter, a typical exposure rate at a 50-cm (19-in.) target-to-table-top distance is 3.5 mR/mAs. At 85 kVp and with a 2.0-mm aluminum filter, the exposure at a 50-cm target-to-panel distance is 1.2 mR/mAs. Therefore, by using added filtration, the exposure reduction to the skin is approximately 65%.

   Regulations require that the **total filtration** permanently in the useful x-ray beam may not be less than **2.5 mm of aluminum equivalent** for image intensification. **Therefore, the intensity of the x-ray beam at the table top should not exceed 2.2 R/min. for each mA of operating tube current at 80 kVp.**

5. **Exposure time**. Operators must restrict the x-ray beam "on" time to a minimum. **Doubling the exposure time also doubles the exposure to the patient.** The x-ray beam need not be operated continuously. Image intensification can be accomplished with a series of short spurts of x-radiation. Five "looks,"

© GR/St. Lucie Press

assuming 12 sec. per look, approximates 1 min. of exposure time. This translates (assuming 5 R/min. exposure) to approximately 400 mR exposure to the patient per "look."

Regulations require that a cumulative manual reset timer be activated by the exposure switch, which may produce an audible signal or temporarily interrupt the x-ray beam. This device is designed to make the operator aware of the relative beam "on" time during each procedure.

6. **Allowable x-ray beam exposure rates** are measured at the panel or table top and shall be as low as practicable. The allowable exposure rates listed below do not apply to magnification procedures or the recording of images where higher exposure rates are required.

Image intensification equipment manufactured after August 1, 1974 equipped with **Automatic Exposure Rate Controls** or **Automatic Brightness Stabilization** shall not be operable at any combination of tube current and potential that will result in an exposure rate in excess of **10 R/min**. at the point where the useful x-ray beam enters the patient (except during recording of images or when an optional high-level control or "boost" position is provided). When the "boost" position or high-level control is used, the equipment shall not be operable at any combination of tube current and potential not to exceed **5 R/min**. The high-level control shall only be operable when continuous manual activation is provided by the operator. A continuous audible signal to the operator shall indicate that the high-level control is being employed.

Image intensification equipment manufactured after August 1, 1974 *without* **Automatic Exposure Rate Controls** or **Automatic Brightness Stabilization** shall not be operable at any combination of tube current and potential that will result in an exposure rate in excess of **5 R/min**. at the point where the center of the useful x-ray beam enters the patient (except during recording of images, or when an

Chapter 7 ■ Factors Affecting Patient and Operator Exposure

optional high-level control or "boost" position controls are activated). The high-level control shall only be operable when continuous manual activation is provided by the operator. A continuous signal audible to the operator shall indicate that the high-level control is being employed.

Devices (meters) that indicate the x-ray tube potential (kVp) and current (mA) must be provided, and should be located, on the generator or image intensifier carriage. Therefore, the operator can monitor the tube potential and current during operation.

California state law requires that when using image intensifiers with AEC or ABS, the operator must monitor the x-ray tube current and potential at least once each week with a designated phantom, of 9 in. of water or 7 7/8 in. of lucite, in the x-ray beam during use to ascertain that the x-ray tube is in normal range for a given set of operating parameters.

The above-mentioned measurements of the table top or patient phantom shall be made at **1 cm** when using an under-the-table x-ray tube and **30 cm** when measuring an overhead x-ray tube.

7. **Target-to-panel distance.** Shorter target-to-panel distance (TPD) results in a greater skin dose to the patient and greater distortion to the image than longer TPDs. Assuming that the exposure rate requirements at the image receptor are the same for both TPDs or automatic exposure rate control, when the TPD is increased from 12 to 18 in., the skin entrance exposure is reduced by approximately 30%. **State laws and the Bureau of Radiologic Health (BRH) require that the target-to-panel or target-to-table-top distance *should not* be less than 18 in. and *shall not* be less than 12 in.**

While the x-ray tube distance can be varied, the image intensifier should always be positioned as close to the patient as possible to maintain low exposures.

8. **Low-absorption table top.** Carbon fiber table tops will significantly reduce patient exposures.

© GR/St. Lucie Press

9. High-level **"BOOST"** fluoroscopy refers to a special activation system that provides a higher tube current, from 10 to 20 mA, and in some instances, 40 mA. The entrance dose rate to the patient is 2 to 10 times higher than conventional fluoroscopy, from 10 to 50 Rads/min. at the table top. These high dose rates are typically used for interventional angiography and cardiography studies, where the need to visualize very small guidewires and catheters requires a higher signal-to-noise ratio and very low amounts of quantum mottle in the image. Recent regulations (1994) limit the **maximum table-top dose rate to 20 Rads/ min. when acquiring images without recording devices, such as video tape.**

   - **Special activation at the control panel is required.**

   - **Audible signal must be heard in the room while the high-level fluoro is energized.**

   - **Table-top dose rate is limited to 20 R/min. unless recording devices are used.**

Review Questions

1. A secondary protective barrier can attenuate _____ radiation.

2. A circuit closing contact by continual pressure is called a _____ switch.

3. With fluoroscopic equipment that has the x-ray tube below the table top, the exposure rate shall be measured at _____ above the table top.

   a. 1 in.

   b. 1 cm

   c. 1 ft

   d. 30 cm

4. For every mA of fluoroscopic technique, one can assume a table-top intensity of

   a. 1 Rad/min.

   b. 2.2 Rad/min.

   c. 0.5 Rad/min.

   d. 1.5 Rad/min.

5. If at 1 ft the intensity is 1,000 R/hr. and you remain there for 6 min., you will receive 100 mR. What would be your exposure if you moved 2 ft away and remained there for 3 min.?

6. The target-to-panel distance of the fluoroscopy unit should not be less than _____ in.

7. The total filtration for the fluoroscopic x-ray tube housing is _____ aluminum equivalent.

8. The fluoroscopic exposure rate without AEC shall not exceed _____.

9. The operator must monitor the fluoroscopic tube current and potential at least _____ during use to ascertain that it is in normal range.

10. When the target-to-panel distance is increased from 12 to 18 in., the skin entrance exposure is reduced by approximately _____%.

11. If the fluoroscopic unit puts out 20 R/hr., how many mR will the fluoroscopist receive in 6 min.?

Answers to the review questions are on page 178. If you answered 8 or more items correctly, go to the next chapter. If you answered fewer than 8 items correctly, reread this chapter and retake the review questions.

Chapter 8

Health Effects of Low-Level X-ray Exposure

Objectives

> Upon completion of Chapter 8, the reader will be able to:
>
> 1. Explain how ionizing radiation may induce somatic changes.
> 2. List the somatic dose indicators such as bone marrow, skin, and thyroid.
> 3. Define genetic dose indicator.
> 4. Define genetically significant dose.

Somatic Dose Indicators

Concern about the effect at the individual level can be expressed in those doses that may induce somatic changes as follows:

1. Injuries to the superficial tissue.
2. Induction of cancer.

3. Other deleterious effects such as cataract formation, impaired fertility, and life-span shortening.

4. Injuries to the developing fetus/embryo.

Most somatic dose indicators are based on measurements of the dose at specific locations, points, or small volumes. The bone marrow, skin, and the thyroid gland are examples of anatomical points and locations that have been used for such measurement. More specifically, the somatic dose indicators are useful in their own right as long as their limitations are understood and are indicative of the major effect. The primary somatic dose indicators are

1. **Bone marrow.** Evaluation of available data suggests that a strong correlation exists between the incidence of leukemia and the mean radiation dose received by the active bone marrow. Furthermore, the bone marrow dose is a reasonable indicator of doses to other internal organs that are sensitive to cancer.

2. **Thyroid and skin.** The measurement of radiation dose to other organs, such as the skin and thyroid, may be useful to determine the probability of certain effects occurring. For example, measurement of the dose to the skin of the anterior chest is a reasonable indicator of the breast dose.

Genetic Dose Indicators

Genetic dose refers to effects exhibited in *future offspring* of persons who have been irradiated. It does not refer to the individual or embryo/fetus that directly receives the radiation exposure. Spermatogonia are drastically depleted by small amounts of radiation (i.e., a dose of 50 mRem delivered in a single brief exposure may result in cessation of sperm).

It is important to note that intense doses on the order of 300 R to the female gonads will produce temporary sterility, while a dose of only 30 R to the testes results in temporary sterility in men.

As one would expect, examinations that expose the gonads/ovaries to primary x-ray beam radiation produce the highest exposures, such as during barium enema examination, IVP, lumbar spine, hips, and upper femur.

When the reproductive cells are irradiated, changes may be produced in the genes or in the chromosomes of these cells, and subsequent generations are referred to as "inherited or genetic effects."

Genetically Significant Dose

The Genetically Significant Dose (GSD) is a factor of three parameters: the function of future children, the x-ray examination rate, and the mean gonadal dose per examination. It can be deduced that the lower the GSD, the lower the number of mutations.

The total estimated Mean Annual Genetically Significant Dose to the U.S. population has been estimated for the year 1970 to be 20 mR, a 20% increase over that of 1964. There is no reason to believe that the trend is not continuing. **It is of interest to note that the lumbar and lumbo-sacral examinations are the largest contributors to the GSD.** Examinations of the thorax account for approximately half of all diagnostic radiographic examinations taken but contribute only a few percent to the total GSD. However, examinations of the abdominal region of the body account for approximately 25% of all radiography but contribute over 70% of the GSD.

Review Questions

1. The mA setting for fluoroscopy is typically less than
   a. 5.
   b. 100.
   c. 10.
   d. 300.

2. The **genetic dose** refers to
   a. effects of radiation on an irradiated person's gonads.
   b. exposure measured by film badges worn at the gonadal level.
   c. effects exhibited in future offspring of persons who have been irradiated.
   d. dose that penetrates gonadal shielding.

3. What is the approximate exposure a patient would receive during 5 min. of fluoroscopy? (Assume one mA of tube current.)
   a. 3 R
   b. 11 R
   c. 60 R
   d. 1 R

4. The bone marrow dose is a reasonable indicator of other internal organs that may be sensitive to _____.
   a. radiation
   b. heat
   c. cancer
   d. all of the above

5. An acute dose of ____ R to the testes will produce temporary sterility in man.

6. A dose of 50 mRem delivered in a single exposure may result in _____.

Answers to the review questions are on page 179. If you answered 4 or more items correctly, go to the next chapter. If you answered fewer than 4 items correctly, reread this chapter and retake the review questions.

Chapter 9

Biological Effects and Significance of X-ray Exposure

Objectives

> Upon completion of Chapter 9, the reader will be able to:
>
> 1. Define cellular amplification.
> 2. Recall the gross cellular effects of radiation.
> 3. Describe the dose effect curves.
> 4. Explain the radiosensitivity of the cell.
> 5. Identify the short-term effects of radiation.
> 6. Identify the long-term effects of radiation—carcinogenic, cataractogenic, and genetic.
> 7. Define stochastic and non-stochastic effects.

Cellular Amplification

Cellular damage at the point of initial radiation interaction usually involves only a very small percentage of total number of molecules in the cell. Therefore, any biological consequences of radiation-induced changes may be relatively insignificant.

Normal cellular metabolic processes may amplify this damage, causing the injury to develop from the molecule to the microscopic level and resulting in possible gross cellular malfunction.

Gross Cellular Effects of Radiation

One of the phenomena seen most frequently in growing tissue exposed to radiation is the cessation of cell division. This may be temporary or permanent depending upon the magnitude of the absorbed dose of radiation. Other criteria observed are chromosome breaks, clumping of chromosome material, formation of giant cells and other mitosis abnormalities, increased granularity of cytoplasm, nuclear disintegration, changes in motility or cytoplasmic activity, vacuolization, altered protoplasmic viscosity, and changes in membrane permeability.

Latent Period

Radiation effects that appear years, decades, and sometimes generations later are referred to as long-term effects.

Dose Effect Curves

Figure 9.1 represents a linear, non-threshold dose effect relationship in which the curve intersects the abscissa at the origin. **According to the non-threshold hypothesis, any dose, no matter how small, is considered to involve some degree of effect. There is some evidence which suggests that the genetic effects of radiation constitute a non-threshold phenomenon.** Under this assumption, some degree of risk is presumed to be present when large populations are exposed to even small amounts of radiation. However, regulatory radiation guides are based on the non-threshold dose effect relationship. Figure 9.1 is a typical sigmoid threshold curve. The point at which the curve intersects the abscissa is the threshold dose.

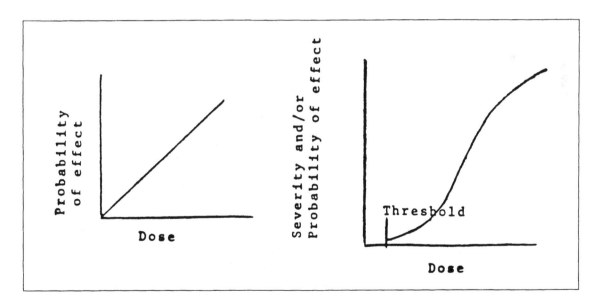

Figure 9.1: Dose effect curves.

Radiosensitivity of the Cell

According to the Law of Bergonie and Tribondeau, the radiosensitivity of tissues depends on the number of undifferentiated cells that the tissue contains, the degree of mitotic activity in the tissue, and the length of time the cells of the tissue stay in active proliferation.

Two French scientists reported that cells which are rapidly dividing, or have a potential for rapid division, are more sensitive than those which do not divide and those which are primitive or unspecialized, such as immature cells. For example, erythroblasts, which are immature red blood cells that have nuclear material, are more radiosensitive than a mature red blood cell, which does not have a nucleus and is more specialized because it carries hemoglobin.

Based on the reported data, it is important to remember that blood-forming organs such as the spleen, bone marrow, gastrointestinal tissue, and the developing embryo/fetus will be more radiosensitive than tissues whose cells have a slower renewal rate.

Various kinds of cells may be grouped as follows in order of diminishing sensitivity:

- Lymphocytes or white blood cells
- Erythrocytes or red blood cells, granulocytes
- Epithelial cells
- Endothelial cells
- Connective tissue cells
- Bone cells
- Nerve cells
- Brain cells
- Muscle cells

Short-Term Effects

In the diagnostic range of ionizing radiation, including image intensification, there is a very small probability of an individual receiving an acute biological effect. The dose range for diagnostic radiography varies from a few milliRads to a few Rads **(1 Rad equals 100 Ergs per gm of tissue)**. However, with image intensification, although the exposure rate seldom exceeds 5 R/min. (measured at the table top), the entire examination may deliver more than 30 Rads. Therefore, image intensification examinations generally deliver greater exposure to the patient and operator than radiographic examinations.

In general, at 25 Rads or less, ordinary laboratory or clinical methods will show no indications of biological injury.

Long-Term Effects

Long-term effects of radiation exposure are those that may manifest years after the original exposure. Delayed radiation effects may result from previous acute, high-dose exposures or from chronic low-level exposure over a period of years. Operators of ionizing radiation equipment, including image intensifiers, must be cognizant of the fact that individuals receiving low chronic exposures over a period of years is a greater concern than the short-term effects of a few individuals receiving a high dose. More specifically, the possibility of genetic damage increases with chronic low-dose radiation.

Carcinogenic Effects

There is human evidence that radiation may contribute to the induction of various kinds of neoplastic disease:

© GR/St. Lucie Press

1. Early radiologists and dentists have shown a significant increase in skin malignancies and leukemia, as compared to physicians who did not use radiation.
2. Radium dial painters, who ingested significant amounts of radioactive radium, have subsequently shown an increased incidence of bone cancer.
3. The Japanese survivors of Hiroshima and Nagasaki have an increased incidence of leukemia and other neoplasia.

The most frequently occurring radiation-induced cancers, in descending order of susceptibility, are the

- Female breast,
- Thyroid gland,
- Hemopoeitic tissue,
- Lungs,
- Gastrointestinal tract, and
- Bones.

Embryological Effects

Considering the fact that immature, undifferentiated, rapidly dividing cells are highly radiosensitive, it is not surprising that embryonic and fetal tissues are highly radiosensitive to even relatively low doses of ionizing radiation. An absorbed dose of even 50 Rads to the fetus could result in an involuntary abortion. In terms of embryonic death, the earliest stages of pregnancy, perhaps a few weeks (preimplantation), are the most radiosensitive. During the second through the sixth week of gestation, the production of biological defects in the newborn is a major consideration. However, in later stages of pregnancy, functional damage, particularly that involving the central nervous system, may result from late exposures. More importantly, biological damage that may result in subtle alterations in such phenomena as

Chapter 9 ▪ Biological Effects and Significance of X-ray Exposure

learning patterns and development may have a considerable latent period before manifestation.

Cataractogenic Effects

The required dose for formation of cataracts is on the order of several hundred Rads (200–250 Rads). The fibers that comprise the lens of the eye are specialized to transmit light. Damage to this tissue and to the developing immature cells of this tissue may result in cataracts.

Clear protective lenses of 0.25 mm lead equivalent will reduce personnel eye radiation exposure by 85–90% during image intensification procedures.

Genetic Effects

The precursor cells of mature gametes or the mature gametes themselves are susceptible to nuclear damage/ genetic mutations from ionizing radiation. Gametes that have altered genetic information can be reproduced and passed on to all of the cells of the offspring.

Animal experimentation remains our chief source of information concerning the genetic effects of irradiation. As a result of extensive experimentation, the following generalizations may be made:

1. There is no indication of a threshold dose for the genetic effects of irradiation.
2. The degree of mutational damage that results from radiation exposure seems to be dose-rate dependent.

Therefore, mutations tend to be deleterious, and it is important to keep the incidence of radiation as low as possible. **More importantly, the goal is clear—Keep the radiation exposure to the gonads at a minimum.**

© GR/St. Lucie Press

Review Questions

1. A dose of _____ Rem/Rad may cause a decrease in the number of leukocytes.

2. Latent biological responses are termed _____ effects.

3. Cells are radiosensitive if they are _____, _____, and _____.

4. Patient dose during image intensification is dependent on_____, _____, and _____.

5. The genetically significant dose is a factor of the following three parameters:

    _____

    _____

    _____

6. If 2 gm of tissue absorb 200 ergs of energy, what is the absorbed dose?

Answers to the review questions are on page 179. If you answered 4 or more items correctly, go to the next chapter. If you answered fewer than 4 items correctly, reread the last 2 chapters and retake the review questions.

Chapter 10

Personnel Radiation Protection

Objectives

Upon completion of Chapter 10, the reader will be able to:

1. Define ALARA.
2. Employ proper operator protection during image intensification procedures.
3. Recall the isoexposure contours during fluoroscopy.
4. Recall the primary fluoroscopic beam attenuation factors.
5. Employ protective devices and accessories such as thyroid shields, overhanging shields, protective curtains, gloves, goggles, and aprons.

ALARA

ALARA is an acronym for "As Low As Reasonably Achievable." ALARA is the philosophy for maintaining occupational radiation exposures as low as reasonably achieved. It must be assumed that there is no minimum threshold of radiation exposure necessary to achieve a biological effect. Even the lowest radiation exposure is assumed to result in some effect, though the effect may be too slight to measure. **It stresses the fact that all radiation exposures to the operator, the staff, and the patient be kept as far below legal limits as possible.**

Operator Exposure

The chief danger to the operator during image intensification procedures is possible exposure to the scattered radiation coming primarily from the patient and, to a lesser degree, other scattering material such as the collimator, x-ray table top, bucky tray, or x-radiation coming from the x-ray tube housing. **The X-ray tube housing must be constructed so that the leakage radiation at a distance of 1 m from the target cannot exceed 100 milliroentgens in 1 hr. when the tube is operated at 80 kVp.**

Operator Protection during Image Intensification Procedures

The operator of the image intensifier should observe the following precautions when he/she is required to remain in the room during the exposure:

1. Stand as far as practicable from the source of scattered radiation (patient).
2. Wear protective aprons of at least 0.25 mm lead equivalent (preferably 0.50 mm) while in the room, if the exposure is likely to be to 5 mR/hr. or more.
3. Monitor the x-ray tube current and potential in the AEC mode at least once each week with a designated phantom during use to ascertain that they are in normal range and keep weekly logs.
4. Wear personnel monitoring devices at the shoulder or collar outside the apron.

© GR/St. Lucie Press

5. Make sure that a bucky slot cover and protective curtain are provided (Figure 10.1).

When the fluoroscopic x-ray tube is operating at 100 kVp, the amount of scattered radiation coming primarily from the patient will be 500 mR/hr. at 1 ft, 100 mR/hr. at 2 ft, and 50 mR/hr. at 3 ft.

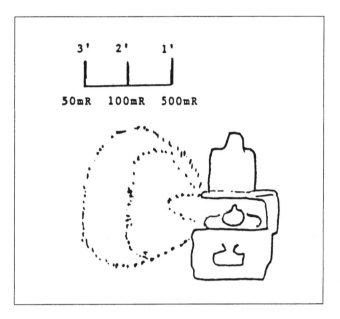

Figure 10.1: Isoexposure profile for a typical image intensifier demonstrating the need for protective curtains and bucky slot covers.

Figure 10.2 depicts the isoexposure contours during image intensification procedures and represents the place (A) where a radiographer and physician could receive the least amount of radiation exposure when they must stay in the room.

Protective Aprons

When the operator is wearing protective clothing, substantial exposure reduction from scattered radiation can be achieved. **A typical exposure reduction is 97%. It is important to remember that scattered and leakage radiation

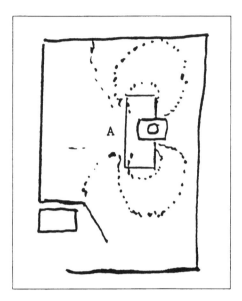

Figure 10.2: Isoexposure profile of a fluoroscopic room.

are of much lower energy than that of the primary beam (Table 10.1). Since lead aprons are generally a barrier to scattered and leakage radiation and not the primary beam, these aprons are quite effective at attenuation.

Table 10.1: Primary Fluoroscopic Beam Attenuation Factors

		mm Pb	% beam attenuation	
kVp	mA	equivalent	normal*	hardened **
50	2	0.25	99.4	92.9
50	2	0.30	99.5	98.0
50	2	0.50	99.9	99.0
50	2	1.00	99.9	99.9
75	2	0.25	96.1	70.0
75	2	0.30	96.7	78.1
75	2	0.50	99.2	88.0
75	2	1.00	99.9	98.2
100	2	0.25	91.4	62.7
100	2	0.30	92.4	70.7
100	2	0.50	97.3	80.3
100	2	1.00	99.6	95.0

* HVL @ 80 kVp, 2 mA: 3.6 mm Al.
** Approximately 2-mm Cu filter added to 50-kVp beam and 4-mm Cu filter added to 75- and 100-kVp beam.
Measurements performed by T.L. Brannon and K. Steward of Valley Sierra Health Services, Sacramento (2/1984) for the Radiologic Health Branch of the California Department of Health Services.

Chapter 10 ▪ Personnel Radiation Protection

During image intensification, operators are generally standing beside the examination table where they can conveniently operate the equipment. The ratio of scattered to incident exposure of x-rays should be remembered by operators and any other personnel who are required to stand near the patient during image intensification procedures.

With an x-ray tube located under the table, the maximum intensities are received above the table-top level at angles of 135° and 120° from the primary beam. In the area below the table, 30° represents the angle where the most intensity is received. The best place for the operator to stand during image intensification exams is at right angles to the patient. The Figure 10.3 best illustrates the intensity distribution during image intensification for an x-ray tube located under the table top.

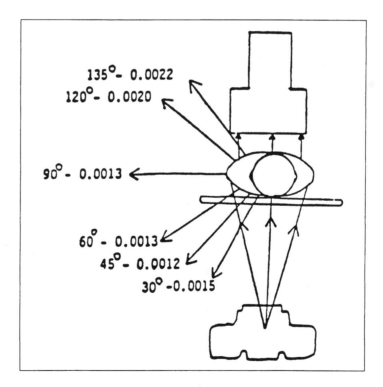

Figure 10.3: The ratio of scattered to incident exposure of x-rays at 100 kVp (National Council on Radiation Protection and Measurements Report No. 49, *Structural shielding design and evaluation for medical use of x-rays and gamma rays of energies up to 10 MeV*, Washington, DC, p. 59).

Other Protective Devices and Accessories

1. **Thyroid shields** of 0.25 mm lead equivalent are available to protect the thyroid gland.

2. **Overhanging shields** that are roof-supported leaded glass and/or lead aprons offer good protection and are more convenient to use than roll-around shields.

3. **Mobile screen desks** usually of 1.0 or 2.0 mm lead equivalent are available.

4. **Protective curtains,** either an overlapping protective curtain or a hinged or sliding panel of at least 0.25 mm lead equivalent, should be positioned between the patient and the operator or others who are required to remain in the room during exposures.

5. **Protective gloves** of 0.25 mm lead equivalent are available.

6. **Lead glass protective goggles and glasses** are available from commercial companies to protect the lens of the eye.

7. **Hangers for protective aprons** should always be used. They help by preventing excessive local strain on the apron or coat shoulders and help to prevent cracking of the lead material, and they make putting the apron on much easier.

Deliberate exposure of an individual to the useful x-ray beam for training purposes or demonstration purposes is not permitted unless there is also a medical indication for the exposure and the radiographic/image intensifier examination was prescribed by a physician.

Review Questions

1. Which of the following is directly proportional to the exposure delivered to the patient?
   a. kilovoltage peak (kVp)
   b. milliamperage (mA)
   c. thickness of the filter
   d. target-to-panel/table-top distance

2. The image intensification operator's exposure to scattered radiation is directly proportional to the _____ exposure.

3. Isoexposure contours during image intensification will show that at a distance of 3 ft from the head of the table, the operator will receive _____.

4. When a C-arm image intensifier is used for an anteroposterior chest view, in which direction is there the most scattered radiation? _____ degrees from the primary beam.

5. When x-ray energy is directed towards the patient, most of the energy is _____.

6. The total filtration for an x-ray tube used for image intensification may not be less than _____mm Al.

7. A diagnostic x-ray tube housing must be so constructed that the leakage radiation at a distance of 1 m from the target cannot exceed _____.

8. The bucky slot cover and protective curtain should have at least _____ equivalent material.

9. The operator must monitor the tube current and potential at least _____.

10. Radiosensitivity of the body is influenced by all of the following *except*
    a. type of radiation and dose rate.
    b. size of the cells.
    c. total dose received by the body.
    d. type of cells being irradiated.

11. Which type of table-top material significantly reduces patient exposure?

Answers to the review questions are on page 179. If you answered 8 or more items correctly, go to the next chapter. If you answered fewer than 8 items correctly, reread the chapter and retake the review questions.

Chapter 11

Personnel Monitoring

Objectives

> Upon completion of Chapter 11, the reader will be able to:
>
> 1. Recall the criteria for using personnel monitoring devices.
> 2. List the types of film badge devices.
> 3. List the advantages and disadvantages of the film badge thermoluminescent dosimeter and pocket ion chamber.
> 4. Define maximum permissible dose.
> 5. Recall the occupational and general public dose equivalent limits.
> 6. Recall the annual occupational dose equivalent.
> 7. Calculate the cumulative occupational dose equivalent.

The largest percentage of exposure to the population from man-made radiation comes from medical and dental x-rays. However, man's senses do not detect ionizing radiation exposure. Therefore, radiation detection devices are designed to measure the radiation level or accumulated exposure to the individual. Ideally, personnel monitoring devices should fulfill at least four criteria:

© GR/St. Lucie Press

113

1. Record the exposure (quantity) to ionizing radiation that has occurred.
2. Measure the accumulated exposure over a specified period of time not to exceed one calendar quarter.
3. Provide some indication of the type and energy (quality) of the incident radiation and the rate at which it was received (acute or chronic).
4. Provide a legally acceptable record of personnel exposure.

Radiation Control Regulations define dose to mean **radiation absorbed per unit mass. A whole body dose** is defined as any exposure to the following:

1. Major portion of the whole body.
2. Head and trunk.
3. Gonads.
4. Lens of the eye.
5. Active blood-forming organs.
6. Whole body.

Any personnel monitoring device reading, unless specifically identified otherwise, is considered to be a *whole body exposure.*

Acceptable personnel monitoring devices are:

1. Film badge.
2. Thermoluminescent dosimeter.
3. Pocket chamber or dosimeter.
4. Audible warning device.

Film Badge

1. Radiation detected: **x-rays, gamma, beta, thermal, and fast neutrons.**
2. Radiation range: **0.01 to 700 Rad.**
3. Minimum energy detected: **10 keV for gamma; 200 keV for beta.**
4. Advantages: **inexpensive, gives estimate of integrated dose, provides a permanent record, provides an objective review, and detects problems.**
5. Disadvantages: **directional dependence, strong energy dependence for low-energy x-rays, and false readings produced by heat, pressure, and certain vapors.**

Thermoluminescent Dosimeter (TLD)

1. Radiation detected: **x-rays, gamma, beta, thermal neutron, and fast neutron.**
2. Radiation range: **10^5 Rad.**
3. Minimum energy detected: **10 keV.**
4. Advantages: **indefinite shelf life within the useful range, small size and low directional dependence, small energy dependence, reusable, and gives estimate of integrated dose over long periods.**
5. Disadvantages: **limited TLD systems supplied as commercial service, cancellation of dose upon reading, dose range dependent on the sensitivity of the reader, radiation detected depends on type of TL material, increased sensitivity with each use, fading, and subjective information of exposure not available.**

Pocket Ionization Chambers

1. Radiation detected: **x-rays, gamma, beta, thermal neutron, and fast neutron.**

2. Radiation range: **0.001 to 2000 Rad. Theoretical for x-ray use: 0.001 to 200 mRad.**

3. Minimum energy detected: **30 keV for gamma rays; 20 keV for fast neutrons.**

4. Advantages: **yield fairly accurate information quickly, small size, low directional dependence, reasonably uniform in response to radiation in the energy range of 50 keV to 2 MeV, economical for long-term use, require little maintenance, and reusable.**

5. Disadvantages: **there is no permanent record; frequent reading, tabulation, and recharging may be required; subject to accidental discharge (through shock and electrical leakage); and range of measurement is limited for each chamber.**

Maximum Permissible Dose (MPD)

The essential aim of radiation safety is to prevent injury from ionizing radiation. Radiation Control Regulations refer to three types of dose equivalent limits:

1. Occupational dose equivalent limits for persons **over** 18 years of age.

2. Occupational dose equivalent limits for persons **under** 18 years of age.

3. Dose equivalent limits for the general population.

4. Prenatal radiation exposure (this may become law in the very near future).

REMEMBER: Radiation exposure received for the operator's own personal medical or dental diagnosis or medical therapy is not considered to be an occupational dose. An operator who is a patient must remove the personnel monitoring device before being x-rayed.

Occupational and General Dose Equivalent Limits

The basic provisions of the Radiation Control Regulations regarding dose equivalent limits are in Rems per **YEAR**. Therefore, 10 CFR 20, section 20.1201 establishes the following **ANNUAL** occupational dose equivalent limits (Table 11.1).

Table 11.1: Annual Occupational Dose Equivalent Limits

BODY AREA	OCCUPATIONAL DOSE	GENERAL PUBLIC
Whole body	5 Rem or 0.05 Sv	0.1 Rem
Extremities	50 Rem or 0.5 Sv	——
Skin of the whole body		
Lens of the eye	15 Rem or 0.15 Sv	

Occupational dose equivalent limits for persons under 18 years of age may receive 10% of the adult occupational dose limits.

Frequency of Exposure Recording

The personnel monitoring devices are worn in order to ensure that the maximum permissible dose equivalent or occupational dose equivalent limits have not been violated. Radiation Control Regulations do not specify the minimum or maximum monitoring time period. Usually, and advisably, film badges or TLD badges are changed once every month.

© GR/St. Lucie Press

Overexposure of a Personnel Monitoring Device

Any reading indicating overexposure of a film badge or other type of dosimeter assigned to an individual is considered to be presumptive evidence of exposure to the individual and must be reported to the Radiologic Health Branch (RHB). Practically all overexposure reports to the RHB resulted from poor working practices of x-ray supervisors and operators who conducted the fluoroscopic examination.

Cumulative Occupational Dose Equivalent

The maximum possible long-term cumulative dose equivalent can be calculated on the basis of 5 Rems/yr. starting at age 18. Therefore, the maximum cumulative whole body dose equivalent is equal to 5 (N – 18), where N is the chronological age in years.

Location of Personnel Monitoring Device

Any personnel monitoring device reading is considered to be whole body dose. Therefore, it may be advisable to wear two or even more personnel monitoring devices. More specifically, for fluoroscopic image intensification or portable image intensification procedures, the personnel monitoring device should always be positioned on the collar above the protective apron or on the top of the protective apron itself. If the exposure under the apron must be determined, as is advisable from time to time, then a second personnel monitoring device should be used.

Who Must Be Monitored

The question of who must be monitored and under what conditions persons must be monitored confronts every x-ray supervisor whose employees run a risk of exposure to radiation. As is often the case with regulations, there are many implied provisions. To a very great extent, this is true with personnel monitoring requirements. Radiation Control Regulations suggest that supervisors should ask themselves: **"Would you, as a Supervisor, want the responsibility of risking any person's safety by not monitoring that person?"**

Those who are not convinced that a realistic and comprehensive monitoring of personnel is advisable should refer to the U.S. Department of Health, Education, and Welfare publication (DMRE 69-3) entitled "Medical Radiation Information for Litigation."

More specifically, there are two other classifications of personnel who must be monitored regardless of the exposure they are likely to receive: persons who enter high radiation areas, and persons who operate mobile x-ray equipment.

There are two broad provisions that deserve emphasis:

1. Each supervisor must take all precautions necessary to provide reasonably adequate protection to the life, health, and safety of all individuals subject to exposure to radiation.
2. Each supervisor is responsible for radiation protection and safety in his/her radiology department, including the use of properly maintained and registered x-ray equipment, the operator's performance, the use of state-authorized operators only, and quality and technical aspects of all x-ray examinations and procedures.

■ Principles of Fluoroscopic Image Intensification and Television Systems: Workbook and Laboratory Manual

Review Questions

1. The occupational whole body dose equivalent for an individual over 18 years of age is _____ per year.

2. Film badges and thermoluminescent dosimeters are changed once each _____.

3. Appropriate personnel monitoring devices shall be worn by individuals 18 years or older who enter a controlled area and may receive _____/hr.

4. The advantages of using a film badge are

    a. _____

    b. _____

    c. _____

    d. _____

5. The possible disadvantages of a pocket dosimeter are

    a. _____

    b. _____

    c. _____

    d. _____

6. A high radiation area is any area accessible to individuals in which there exists radiation at such levels that an individual could receive in any 1 hr. a dose to the whole body in excess of _____.

7. If at 1 ft from the radiation source the intensity of the exposure is 240 mR/hr. and you remain at this location for 10 min., you will receive an exposure of 40 mR. What would be your exposure if you moved 2 ft away from the radiation source and remained there for 20 min.?

> **Answers to the review questions are on page 179. If you answered 5 or more items correctly, go to the next chapter. If you answered fewer than 5 items correctly, reread the chapter and retake the review questions.**

120   © GR/St. Lucie Press

Chapter 12

Pediatric Fluoroscopy

Objectives

> Upon completion of Chapter 12, the reader will be able to:
>
> 1. Describe ways in which to minimize motion for pediatric fluoroscopy.
> 2. List personnel and parental protection techniques during pediatric fluoroscopy.
> 3. Apply gonadal shielding when appropriate.
> 4. Identify the effects of automatic exposure control problems that may occur for pediatric fluoroscopic procedures.

The radiation dose received by children for image intensification examinations is generally significantly less than those received by adults for an equivalent study. However, the longer life span of a child allows more time for manifestation of long-term detrimental effects of radiation. More importantly, as the Law of Bergonie and Tribondeau suggests, children would generally be more sensitive to the effects of radiation since their young tissues undergo higher rates of mitotic activity than those of adults.

© GR/St. Lucie Press

More specifically, it is especially important to keep radiation doses to children to a minimum, particularly during image intensification, since these procedures give much larger doses of radiation to the patient than radiography. Image intensification should only be performed if radiography cannot provide the necessary information.

Motion

Motion accounts for more imaging problems during image intensification with children. Whenever possible, establishing a friendly, non-threatening rapport with the child in order to obtain optimum cooperation is quite worthwhile. Practicing the necessary breath-holding or position-changing required during the procedure will prevent unnecessary radiation exposure. Depending on the child's age, however, he/she may be incapable of understanding instructions to remain motionless for the required period of time necessary for the examination. In some cases, where long examination periods are necessary or when the exam itself is particularly uncomfortable, it may be necessary to use anesthesia or sedation. There are several methods of achieving mechanical mobilization.

Mechanical means of securing infants and small children are available commercially or may be easily made. These devices range from simple boards with Velcro straps to more complex positioning aids that move in a variety of angles and positions. The use of sandbags and compression bands has also been found useful.

Personnel and Parental Protection

There are many situations where it is impossible to employ mechanical methods of immobilization and not medically practical to use sedation or anesthesia or when sterile conditions must be maintained. In such cases, hospital personnel or parents must physically restrain the infant or toddler during the radiation exposure. It is important to remember that the scattered radiation from image intensification examinations can be significant for those standing near the patient. Therefore, lead gloves and aprons should be worn by whoever holds the patient and all other personnel who are standing in close proximity to the patient. When hospital personnel are frequently involved in holding patients, their exposures should be carefully monitored.

Gonadal Shielding

Gonadal shielding of at least 0.5 mm lead equivalent must be used whenever possible when it does not interfere with the examination. It is very important to use gonadal shielding for children. The genetic effects of radiation are thought to be cumulative. Therefore, it is absolutely necessary to protect the children's gonads from radiation that may produce deleterious effects in their offspring.

Automatic Exposure Control (AEC)

Automatic Exposure Control (AEC) is particularly valuable for use in children's image intensification examinations since choosing the correct exposure factors is much more difficult for children than adults. It is important to note that AEC will not function properly unless the child covers the entire detection device. Therefore, using AEC for infants and very small children may not be possible. However, when radiopaque structures are in the exposed field of the AEC, exposure controls will increase the radiation exposure to the maximum.

Other Technical Considerations

Using the smallest beam size and keeping the patient-to-image intensifier distance as short as possible are extremely important technical considerations. Adjusting the cineradiographic framing rates to the minimum necessary for the examination will reduce patient exposures. Grids are not necessary when exposing infants since there is a small volume being irradiated. Using a spot-film camera instead of the spot-film device will reduce the exposure significantly. The spot-film camera allows for the use of shorter exposure times, which decreases motion blurring.

Review Questions

1. Gonadal shielding of at least ____ lead equivalent must be used whenever possible.

2. The tissues of young children are more radiosensitive since the tissue has a higher rate of _____ than adults.

3. Immobilizing children may be accomplished by
   a. friendly rapport.
   b. mechanical devices.
   c. sedation.
   d. all of the above.

4. What is the absorbed dose if 200 ergs of energy were absorbed in 2 gm of tissue?

5. If the x-ray tube intensity is 25 R/hr., what is the intensity for 15 min. of fluoroscopy time?

6. Which recording device will significantly reduce the exposure to a child?
   a. spot-film device
   b. spot-film camera
   c. both will be the same exposure

Answers to the review questions are on page 179. If you answer 4 or more items correctly, go the next chapter. If you answered fewer than 4 items correctly, reread the chapter and retake the review questions.

Chapter 13

Mobile Image Intensification Equipment

Objectives

Upon completion of Chapter 13, the reader will be able to:

1. Describe the type of structural shielding that is required for mobile fluoroscopic procedures.
2. Recall the equipment provisions for mobile C-arm.
3. Use image storage video disc recording to reduce patient exposure.

Structural Provisions

Structural shielding required for mobile image intensification units is employed for scattered radiation and is generally minimal. The entire primary beam is intercepted by the image receptor. However, there are certain regulatory provisions that should be noted.

© GR/St. Lucie Press

127

1. When mobile equipment is to be used routinely in one location, shielding must be provided as for a fixed installation.

2. When mobile equipment is routinely used in operating rooms, appropriate structural shielding must be provided for these rooms.

Equipment Provisions (Mobile C-Arm)

1. Inherent provisions must be made so that the machine cannot be operated at a source-to-skin distance of less than 30 cm or 12 in.

2. Image intensification must be provided.

3. Conventional fluoroscopic screens are not permitted.

4. It shall be impossible to operate the image intensifier when the collimating cone or diaphragm is not in place.

5. It shall be impossible to energize the useful beam of a mobile unit unless the entire useful beam is intercepted by the image receptor.

6. The maximum dose rate of five (5) Roentgens per minute may not be exceeded as measured at 30 cm from the input surface of the image assembly.

7. Personnel monitoring is required for all persons operating mobile image intensification equipment.

8. Protective aprons of at least 0.25 mm lead equivalent must be worn if a person is likely to receive 5 mR/hr. or more.

When observation of actual motion is not needed, such as in most orthopedic examinations or urological examinations and parts of some surgical cardiac procedures, operators of mobile image intensification equipment may incorporate an image storage video disc recorder with electronic radiography. THIS OPERATION WILL SIGNIFICANTLY REDUCE PATIENT DOSE.

Boost Position (High-Level Control Button)

When the boost position, or the high-level control button, is provided on a mobile fluoroscope, it will increase the maximum x-ray exposure level. The correct way to employ this option is to first use the normal mode to locate the area of interest, then to use the boost position only when it is necessary to achieve the quality of image required.

Mobile Fluoroscope Quality Control

With a mobile fluoroscope (C-arm) with manual exposure control, the operator shall monitor the x-ray tube current and potential at least once each day during use to ascertain that the x-ray tube is within normal range. A written log shall be kept of all monitored readings and shall include at least the tube current and potential, the date, identification of the mobile C-arm, and the name of the person who did the monitoring. Radiation measurements of the table top or patient exposure rate shall be made at least once each year for units with automatic exposure control, at least once every three years for units without automatic exposure control, and immediately following the alteration or replacement of a major component such as the x-ray tube, the exposure controls, the imaging assembly, or the power source.

Review Questions

1. Each frame of a television picture consists of _____ scan lines.

2. How long does it take the fluoroscopic table to move from the horizontal to the vertical position?

3. What is the minification ratio of a 14-in. image intensification tube?

4. List the various types of secondary barriers.

   _____

   _____

   _____

   _____

5. The intensity of the x-ray beam at the table top shall not exceed _____ for each mA of tube current at 80 kVp.

Answers to the review questions are on page 179. If you answered 3 or more items correctly, go to the next chapter. If you answered fewer than 3 items correctly, reread the chapter and retake the review questions.

Chapter 14

California Radiation Control Regulations: Responsibility of the Supervisor and Operator

Objectives

Upon completion of Chapter 14, the reader will be able to:

1. List the four groups of individuals who may expose humans to radiation in California.
2. Recall the restrictions of holders of a certificate of permit in radiologic technology.
3. Recall the record keeping requirements for California.
4. Describe the incident notification requirements for the California Department of Health Services.
5. Recall the required training and information provided to x-ray users.
6. Employ the California State Requirements for Supervision of Radiologic Technology Personnel.
7. Operate the fluoroscopic equipment in compliance with state and national regulatory provisions.
8. Calculate the inverse square law formula.
9. Identify patient scheduling criteria for women of child-bearing years.

© GR/St. Lucie Press

131

■ Principles of Fluoroscopic Image Intensification and Television Systems: Workbook and Laboratory Manual

> 10. Identify parameters for occupational women of procreative years.
> 11. Understand the importance of using gonadal shielding.
> 12. Identify the basic types of gonadal shielding.

Any person possessing an X-ray Operator and Supervisor permit is subject to a wide variety of state and federal laws and appropriate regulations. In some instances, they may also be subjected to county statutes and ordinances regarding radiation safety.

Except for stated exemptions, only persons who possess proper, valid, and up-to-date certificates or permits issued by states are authorized to expose human beings to x-rays for diagnostic purposes. There are four distinct groups of individuals who may expose humans to x-radiation in California:

1. Licentiates of the healing arts (M.D., D.O., D.P.M., D.C.) who possess one of the following authorizations may expose human beings to x-radiation within the limits of their professional licenses:

   a. **Radiology Supervisor and Operator Certificates.** American Board of Radiology or American Osteopathic Board of Radiology certified physicians whose practice is limited to radiology, including image intensification.

   b. **Fluoroscopy Supervisor and Operator Permit.** Licentiates who actuate or energize fluoroscopic image intensification equipment themselves or directly control radiation exposure to the patient during the procedure or supervise radiologic technologists who hold a valid fluoroscopy permit.

   c. **Radiography Supervisor and Operator Permit.** Licentiates who activate or energize radiographic

132 © GR/St. Lucie Press

equipment themselves or supervise radiologic technologists or limited permit technicians who perform radiographic examinations.

d. **Dermatology Supervisor and Operator Permit.** Licentiates who use low-level x-ray treatment for skin diseases only.

2. Certified Diagnostic Radiologic Technologists (CRTs) who have at least two years of formal schooling or training and have qualified for the CRT certification may perform radiographic examinations. CRTs who possess fluoroscopy permits pursuant to section 30451 may also perform image intensification procedures.

3. Limited Permit X-ray Technicians, who have had less than two years of x-ray training prescribed and approved by the state, may perform radiographic procedures restricted to certain areas of the body. **Limited Permit X-ray Technicians are prohibited from performing fluoroscopic image intensification procedures.**

4. Students in approved radiologic technology programs under state-approved supervision of a CRT may perform radiographic procedures. **Students are prohibited from performing fluoroscopic image intensification procedures.**

Restrictions

X-ray supervisors and operators may expose human beings to x-radiation and supervise the activities of technologists or limited permittees only within the scope of their professional licenses. For example, a podiatrist may not supervise activities of a CRT if the CRT is taking other than podiatric examinations.

© GR/St. Lucie Press

Limited permit x-ray technicians may not perform radiographic procedures that are not specifically allowed by their permit.

Restrictions pertaining to holders of a certificate or a permit in radiologic technology are as follows:

1. They may use x-ray equipment only under the supervision of a certified supervisor and operator.
2. They may not interpret any radiograph or make a diagnosis based upon it or the fluoroscopic image to a patient except as ordered by a licentiate of the healing arts.
3. They may not use any title or designation implying or indicating the right to practice any of the healing arts.

Display of Documents

Section 30404 (g) requires that each x-ray supervisor and operator permit, certified radiologic technologist certificate, or technologist fluoroscopy permit must be prominently displayed in the place of employment. If a person is employed by more than one facility in an x-ray supervisor and operator capacity, a photocopy of their permit must also be displayed at each additional place of employment.

A current copy of the California Radiation Control Regulations and a copy of operating procedures applicable to working with x-ray machines and procedures must be posted or must be readily available to each x-ray operator under a supervisor's jurisdiction.

A current copy of Department Form RH-2364 *Notice to Employees* must be posted. Copies of Form RH-2364 may be obtained from the Department.

Record Keeping Requirements

Each user is required to maintain current and complete records, according to section 30293 (a) as follows:

1. The results of each required calibration, survey, and test.
2. Each receipt, transfer, and disposal of a source of radiation.
3. Radiation exposure of all individuals for whom personnel monitoring is required.

The exposure records must be kept on the Department of Health Form RH-2365 or in a manner that includes all of the applicable information required on that form.

Each personnel monitoring entry must be for a period of time not exceeding one calendar quarter. Dose equivalents must be recorded in Rems or millirems and dose equivalent rates in Rems or millirems per hour.

Each required record of dose equivalent received by individuals and of medical examinations must be kept (preserved) indefinitely. Other required documents must be preserved for a period of three years following the date of that occurrence that is the subject of such record.

Incident Notification Requirements

The State Department of Health Services must be notified when individuals are exposed to radiation, for other than prescribed medical purposes, in excess of the limits set forth in the regulations. Immediate notification means a prompt reporting by telephone (916-445-6265) and confirmation by letter to the California State Department of Health Services. Twenty-four-hour notification means telephoning the Department within 24 hours of the prompt confirming letter of the incident. Thirty-day notification means reporting in writing to the State Department of Health Services within the time period.

Required Training and Information Provided to X-ray Users

It is the responsibility of each x-ray supervisor and operator to provide to all x-ray operators under their jurisdiction all of the following:

1. Safety rules to each individual operating x-ray equipment under his/her control. These safety rules must include any restrictions of the operating techniques required for safe operation of the particular x-ray apparatus, and the user must require that the operator demonstrate familiarity with these rules.

2. Instruct all individuals employed as x-ray technologists in the health protection problems associated with exposure to radiation.

3. Instruct in precautions and procedures to minimize exposure to both the patient and the operator.

4. Instruct in the purpose and functions of protective devices employed such as gonadal shielding, protective apparel, collimation, etc.

5. Instruct all individuals to observe applicable regulations of the Department of Health Services.

6. Instruct all x-ray technologists of their responsibility to report promptly to the registered user any condition that may lead to or cause a violation of the California Radiation Control Regulations.

7. Instruct all individuals to wear personnel monitoring devices.

8. Advise individuals as to their radiation exposures.

X-ray Equipment Safety Provisions

No user shall operate or permit the operation of x-ray equipment unless the equipment and installation meet the applicable requirements of the California Radiation Control Regulations and are appropriate for the procedures to be performed.

In order to ensure compliance with the California Radiation Control Regulations, persons authorized by the State Department of Health Services are permitted, without a warrant, at all reasonable times, to inspect each user's x-ray machines, activities, facilities, premises, and records pertaining to radiography and/or fluoroscopy image intensification and associated supervising activities.

Supervision of Radiologic Technology Personnel

It is the responsibility of x-ray supervisors to ascertain that the technologists under their jurisdiction possess proper, up-to-date, valid authorizations issued by the California State Department of Health Services. Radiographic certificates are required to expose human beings to radiographic procedures. Fluoroscopy permits are required if technologists position the patient or select technical factors or exposures to the patient during fluoroscopic procedures.

Since there are restrictions as to the scope of a certificate or permit, it is the supervisor's responsibility to ascertain that no technologist work out-of-scope of their certificates or permits.

Supervision is defined as the responsibility for, and control of, radiation protection and safety, including the use of properly maintained and registered x-ray equipment, the performance of technologists, the use of state-authorized technologists only, and the quality and technical aspects of all x-ray examinations and procedures.

As a Fluoroscopy Supervisor and Operator, it is the physician's responsibility to ascertain that all x-ray technologists under his/her jurisdiction comply with all of the following:

1. Know exactly which examination the technologist is to make before the exposure is made.
2. Clear the fluoroscopy room of all non-essential persons prior to generating x-rays.
3. Collimate the useful beam to the area of clinical interest.
4. Use gonadal shielding where appropriate.
5. Use correct technique factors, optimum kVp, and lowest mA possible for low-dose fluoroscopy consistent with obtaining a diagnostic quality image.
6. Position the patient correctly for the requested examination before making the actual exposure.
7. Take steps to avoid patient motion by carefully instructing the patient not to move, by using appropriate immobilization or positioning aids, and by keeping the patient comfortable and under constant observation.

Insist that positive proof of collimation and gonadal shielding, if indicated, are present on all images.

Fluoroscopic equipment should be in compliance with state and national regulatory provisions at all times. Satisfactory operation of all x-ray equipment should be checked periodically. More importantly, radiologic technologists should observe a number of precautions to reduce their own personal radiation exposure as follows:

1. A lead apron must be worn by each person (except the patient) in the exam room when fluoroscopy is being performed. The personnel monitoring device should be fastened to the outside of the apron at the

shoulder level. During image intensification, the radiologic technologist should remain behind the protective barrier, or if that is not possible, should stand as far from the table as practicable or behind the fluoroscopist.

2. A technologist must remain at least 6 ft from the patient, away from the primary x-ray beam, during portable examinations. A lead apron or a portable lead shield must be provided.

3. Additional personnel protective devices should be worn.

Technologists' Fluoroscopy Clinical Instruction

1. The supervisor shall offer competency-based supervised clinical instruction and education, which shall be completed within one year following completion of didactic instruction and shall include at least the following hours of specialized instruction in fluoroscopic positioning

   - Gastrointestinal tract: 3 hours

   - Vascular/angio systems: 3 hours

   - Orthopedic procedures: 3 hours

2. **The supervisor shall issue a clinical training completion document to all technologists who have successfully completed competency-based clinical education. Refer to Appendix B for a sample Statement of Competency/Technologist's Use of Fluoroscopy Equipment.**

   All activity in an x-ray department should be so designed, procedures so established, and the supervision activities so conducted as to achieve the maximum diagnostic information from fluoroscopic examinations, while at the same time minimizing the exposure to the patient, the operator, and all others.

© GR/St. Lucie Press

Reduction in Dose

There are three basic principles, which can be used separately or in combination, to reduce the dose to X-radiation:

1. Time: keep the time of the x-ray procedure as short as possible.
2. Distance: keep the distance between the source of exposure and the exposed individual as large as practicable.
3. Shielding: insert shielding material between the source of radiation and the exposed person.

Time

During image intensification examinations, the dose to the patient is directly related to the dose rate and the duration of the exposure. The operator exposure to scattered radiation is directly proportional to patient exposure. The cumulative manual reset timer has been specifically designed to make the fluoroscopist aware of the relative x-ray beam "on" time during each fluoroscopic procedure.

Distance

The intensity of radiation varies inversely as the square of the distance. It is obvious that as the distance from the x-ray source increases, the less radiation dose per unit of time people will receive. More specifically, the target-to-panel distances on the image intensifier are usually as long as practicable (should be 18 in.).

The inverse square law is defined as follows:

At points distant from a common source of x-radiation, the intensities of radiation at these points vary as the square of their respective distances from the x-ray source. As one moves farther away from the x-ray source, the radiation received will be less since the x-ray beam diverges as it moves away from the point source. The inverse square law can be expressed in the following mathematical relationship:

$$\frac{I_1}{I_2} = \frac{(d_2)^2}{(d_1)^2}$$

Shielding

Shielding is one of the most important principles for radiation protection. Shielding refers to the different means used to stop radiation or to prevent exposure to it. To be able to apply shielding methods, one must have some understanding of the manner in which x-radiation is attenuated (absorbed) in an absorbing medium. Energy is lost three ways:

1. A photoelectric effect, which is a collision between a photon of x-radiation and an orbital electron of an atom where the electron is knocked out of its orbit and the photon looses all its energy.

2. Compton scatter, which is an interaction of a photon of x-radiation with an orbital electron of the absorber atom, producing a recoil electron and a photon energy which is less than that of the incident photon.

3. Pair production, which is an incident in which a photon is annihilated in the vicinity of the nucleus of the absorbing atom with subsequent production of an electron and a positron.

Scheduling Radiologic Examinations for Women of Child-Bearing Years

Radiology literature suggests that there is no time period during which a radiology examination can be conducted with NO biological risk accruing to the real or potential embryo/fetus or to a future fertilized ovum. This statement is predicated on three assumptions:

1. There is always a small potential for adverse biological effects to occur following exposure to x-radiation.
2. There is no threshold for such effects.
3. Such effects are linearly proportional to absorbed radiation dose.

Major adverse effects include leukemia, congenital malformations, cancer induction, resorption or death of the embryo, and genetic considerations.

Since there is no absolute "safe" period for the conduction of diagnostic x-ray examinations in fertile women, the Radiologic Health Sciences Education Project of the University of California, San Francisco, has reported:

Diagnostic x-ray examinations that have been requested or performed after full consideration of the clinical status of the patient, including the possibility of pregnancy, need not be postponed or selectively scheduled except in those few instances where the examination may not be related to the patient's current illness.

This statement is not substantially different from the 10- and 14-day rule that is suggested by the ICRP and NCRP, which states that 10 or 14 days after the onset of menses, it is improbable that a women would be pregnant, and, therefore, these are "safer" times to perform x-ray examinations. The primary difference is in the emphasis of the guidance. More importantly, modification of an examination to reduce radiation dose can be considered. Diagnostic examinations can be very thorough and detailed in order to provide maximum information.

Therapeutic Abortions

Another important issue to consider in diagnostic radiology is the question of whether or not therapeutic abortions should be recommended and performed because of exposure of the embryo/fetus to diagnostic levels of x-radiation. The Radiologic Health Sciences Education Project has investigated and concluded that

Interruption of pregnancy is never justified from radiation exposure to the fetus/embryo during a diagnostic x-ray examination. This includes exposures from both abdominal and peripheral examinations.

The rationale for this conclusion is based on the fact that if a therapeutic abortion were performed on each woman who has received an abdominal x-ray examination, the result would be the sacrifice of approximately 1,000 normal fetuses to save the birth of one possible abnormal child. This is a conservative estimate in that the actual value may be 1 in 200 or even as high as 1 in 10,000 depending on the specific situation.[1]

The National Council on Radiation Protection and Measurements (NCRP) report #54 establishes the following:

The risk to the embryo/fetus is considered to be negligible at 5 Rad or less when compared to the other risks of pregnancy, and the risk of malformations is significantly increased above control levels only at doses above 15 Rad. Therefore, the exposure of the fetus to radiation arising from diagnostic procedures would very rarely be cause for terminating a pregnancy. If there are reasons other than the possible radiation effects to consider a therapeutic abortion, such reasons should be discussed with the patient by the attending physician, so that it is clear that the radiation exposure is not being used as an excuse for terminating the pregnancy.

NCRP recommendations state that the fetal exposure to diagnostic radiation "would rarely be cause in itself for terminating a pregnancy."

Occupationally Exposed Women of Procreative Age

Section 30280 (b) (1) of the California Radiation Control Regulations establishes that each user must instruct occupationally exposed individuals in the health protection problems associated with radiation. A special situation arises with occupationally exposed women. NCRP report #39 indicates that special precautions should be taken to limit exposure to young women, especially if they could be pregnant.

Certified supervisors are responsible for informing employees of the following:

1. The NCRP has recommended that, during the entire gestation period, the maximum permissible dose equivalent to the fetus from occupational exposure of the expectant mother should not exceed 0.5 Rem (500 mRem).
2. Reasons for the recommendation.

The following facts should be given to female employees:

© GR/St. Lucie Press

1. The first three months of pregnancy are the most important since the embryo/fetus is most sensitive to radiation at this time.

2. In most cases of occupational exposure, the actual dose received by the embryo/fetus is less than the dose received by the mother because some of the dose is absorbed by the mother's body.

3. At the present occupational dose equivalent limits, the risk to the unborn baby is considered to be small, but experts disagree on the exact amount of risk.

4. There is no need for women to be concerned about sterility or loss of the ability to bear children.

5. The NCRP recommendation of 0.5 Rem (500 mRem) dose equivalent limit applies to the full 9 months of pregnancy.

The supervisor should also advise the employee of the following options available to her:

1. Delay having children as long as one works around radiation.

2. Resign from the job. If this is a realistic option, it should be done immediately since the embryo/fetus is most sensitive to radiation at the onset of pregnancy.

3. Request temporary reassignment to tasks that involve less risk of being exposed to radiation.

4. Use a protective apron while exposing patients.

5. Never hold patients.

6. Do not perform portable or surgical x-ray examinations.

7. Do not assist in special procedures or fluoroscopic image intensification procedures.

8. Whenever possible, stay out of the x-ray room and behind protective barriers while the x-ray beam is activated.

Summary of Gonad Shielding in Diagnostic Radiology

A gonad shield is any material placed between the x-ray source and the gonads that attenuates radiation to the required degree. The main purpose is to protect the gonads from exposure to primary x-ray beam. The use of gonadal shielding in California is mandatory, as is the restriction of the x-ray beam to the area of clinical interest.

Gonad shields are of three basic types: flat contact shields, shaped contact shields, and shadow shields.

1. Flat contact shields. These consist of uncontoured, lead-impregnated material, placed on or taped to the patient to cover the gonads. This type of shield is most effective for AP or PA views where the patient is recumbent. Since flat contact shields are difficult to secure in place, they are not well suited to image intensification procedures or non-recumbent procedures.

2. Shaped contact shields. These consist of radiopaque material contoured to enclose the male gonads. Recently, shaped contact shields have become commercially available that can be contained within various carriers such as athletic supports, for upright standing positions. This feature makes this shield acceptable for use during selected image intensification procedures.

3. Shadow shields. A shadow shield consists of some radiopaque material, suspended over the patient's body to cast a "shadow" in the primary beam over the area of the gonads. Shadow shields offers the advantage of use in a sterile field and for use with incapacitated patients.

4. A 0.5 mm lead equivalent gonadal shield will reduce the gonad dose by 97%. **With an x-ray beam of 100 kVp and 3 mm of aluminum filtration, the transmission through the shield is 3%.**

According to the U.S. Department of HEW publication *Specific Area Gonadal Shielding*, Paragraph 1000.50 (A) recommends that specific area gonad shielding be used if the gonads of the patient lie within the primary beam or within close proximity (about 5 cm), even with proper x-ray beam collimation.

The following guidelines are listed in the *Federal Register*, July 23, 1976, 41(143):

1. Specific area testicular shielding should always be used during those examinations in which the testes usually are in the primary beam, such as examinations of the pelvis and upper femur or other examinations where the testes could not be excluded from the primary x-ray beam.

2. Specific area testicular shielding may also be warranted during abdominal and abdominal scout films for barium enema and upper GI series. Each x-ray facility should evaluate its procedures, techniques, and equipment. More importantly, it should establish guidelines as to when testicular shielding should be provided routinely.

3. Specific area gonad shielding should never be used as a substitute for careful patient positioning, the use of correct technique factors and film processing, or proper x-ray beam limitation (collimation).

4. Specific area gonad shielding should provide attenuation of x-rays at least equivalent to that afforded by 0.50 mm of lead.

    Specific area gonad shielding should be used only if the clinical objective of the examination will not be compromised.

    a. The decision concerning the applicability of shielding for an individual patient is dependent upon consideration of the patient's characteristics and the diagnostic information needed of the examination.

b. While in many instances, ovarian shielding is impractical, it may be possible to use the specific area ovarian shielding during selected views in some examinations.

Visual Physiology

The eye contains two types of light receptors—rods and cones. Cones function in daylight or in **photocopic vision**, while the rods function in night or **scotopic vision**. Cones perceive color while rods perceive grays. Both of these structures are found in the retina. The cones are concentrated on the center of the retina whereas the rods are concentrated on the periphery of the retina. This physiologic arrangement (Figure 14.1) explains why dimly lit objects are seen better when viewed peripherally and when they are not looked at directly.

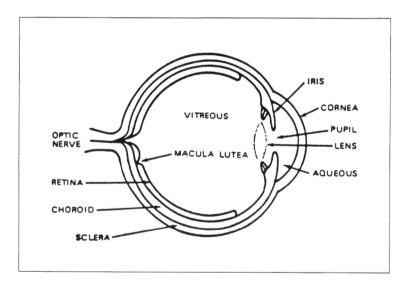

Figure 14.1: Visual physiology.

The ability to perceive fine detail is called **visual acuity**. The visual acuity of rods is poor compared to that of cones, which require daylight levels of light in order to function. Photopic visual acuity is about 10 times greater than scotopic acuity. Therefore, it is important to obtain high image brightness with the use of image intensifiers that bring the illumination of the image into the cone vision region, dramatically improving visual acuity.

For image-intensified fluoroscopy, the room lighting should be dim to enhance visualization of the black and white television images. Excessive light decreases the ability of the eye to resolve detail on the television screen and, therefore, may indirectly cause the operator to change technical factors to produce a brighter image. Increasing the technical factors (mA, kVp) will directly affect patient radiation dose.

The normal viewing distance of an image is **12 to 15 in.** The time required by the eye for recognition of an image (integration time) is **0.2 sec.** Therefore, if a fluoroscopic image is not bright enough for diagnostic imaging purposes, prolonged observation will not improve it.

The room lighting would be dim to enhance visualization of the black and white television images. Excessive light decreases the ability of the eye to resolve detail on the television screen and, therefore, may indirectly cause the operator to change the technical factors to produce a brighter image. **Increasing the technical factors will directly affect patient exposure.**

Provisions must be made to eliminate extraneous light that interferes with the fluoroscopic examination.

Half Value Layer (HVL)

Half value layer is used in two different situations:

1. Determining the barrier thickness, which is the amount of shielding needed to attenuate radiation to the required degree.
2. Determining the quality that is the average penetrating ability of an x-ray beam.

The quality of an x-ray beam is usually specified in terms of half value layer (HVL). **The HVL is defined as the thickness or layer of a specified material that attenuates the x-ray beam to such an extent that the exposure rate is reduced to one half.**

It is commonly expressed in millimeters thickness of aluminum. A higher HVL for an x-ray beam means that it can penetrate a given thickness of material, including human tissue, to a greater extent than a lower HVL layer.

The barrier thickness is usually expressed in terms of inches or millimeters of a specified material, usually lead, required to attenuate radiation to a specified energy to a degree where a person, on the other side of that barrier, will not be exposed to greater than permissible amounts of radiation.

Endnote

1. The information presented is excerpted from papers presented by Reynold F. Brown, M.D., John W. Shaver, M.S., and David A. Lamel, Ph.D. of the Radiologic Health Science Project, University of California, San Francisco.

Chapter 14 ▪ California Radiation Control Regulations: Responsibility of the Supervisor and Operator

Review Questions

1. Horizontal television resolution is controlled by the _____ _____.

2. What are the three basic principles of occupational radiation protection?

   _____

   _____

   _____

3. A 0.5-mm Pb gonadal shield will reduce the gonad dose by _____%.

4. The ability of the eye to perceive fine detail is called_____ _____.

5. The normal binocular viewing distance of an image is _____in.

6. Excessive light _____ the ability of the eye to resolve detail.
   a. decreases
   b. increases

7. If 4 mm of aluminum is required to reduce the x-ray beam intensity from 250 mR to 125 mR, what is the half value layer?
   a. 2 mm Al
   b. 4 mm Al
   c. 8 mm Al
   d. none of the above

> **Answers to the review questions are on page 180. If you answered 5 or more items correctly, go to the next chapter. If you answered fewer than 5 items correctly, reread the chapter and retake the review questions.**

© GR/St. Lucie Press

Chapter 15

Three-Dimensional Fluorographic Anatomy

Objectives

> Upon completion of Chapter 15, the reader will be able to:
>
> 1. Collect information to assist the radiographer in performing fluoroscopic procedures.
> 2. Interpret criteria necessary for competency in fluoroscopic operation for patient procedures.
> 3. Describe the three methods for fluoroscopic localization techniques.
> 4. Identify fluoroscopic anatomy and patient positions for gallbladder, terminal ileum, and knee arthrography.

Fluoroscopic Localization Techniques

The fluoroscopic localization techniques are the (1) parallax method, (2) right-angle method, and (3) radiopaque method.

© GR/St. Lucie Press

The **parallax method** is based on the principle that the images cast by two objects equidistant from the fluoroscopic screen will move together at the same amplitude when the fluoroscope and tube are simultaneously moved back and forth across them. A metal indicator (a sponge forceps) is used for parallax localization of the depth of foreign bodies.

After locating the foreign body, the fluoroscopist closes the diaphragm shutters down to the size of the object to direct the central ray through its center. He/she marks the skin or tapes a suitable metallic marker in position to indicate the exact site of the foreign body in the frontal plane. He/she then places the metal indicator against the side of the body and, holding it in an exactly horizontal position, moves the screen back and forth as he/she raises or lowers the indicator until the images of the foreign body and the indicator move at the same amplitude. He/she then marks the side of the body to indicate the depth of the foreign body.

The parallax method is the method of choice when the patient cannot be turned for right-angle projections. It may also be used for depth localization in such regions as the shoulder, buttocks, and upper thigh.

The **right-angle method** is applicable when turning the patient is not contraindicated by his/her condition or by the nature or location of the foreign body. It simply consists of locating and suitably marking the exact site of the foreign body in the frontal plane and then repeating the procedure with the patient in the lateral position.

The **radiopaque method** requires the use of contrast media to coat the object or localize the site of an obstruction, opaque foreign body, and/or calculus.

Gallbladder Fluoroscopy

The biliary system consists of the bile ducts and gallbladder. The two main ducts emerge at the porta hepatic and join to form the common hepatic duct which unites with the cystic duct to form the common bile duct. The gallbladder is a thin-walled, pear-shaped musculomembranous sac with a capacity of storing 2 oz. of bile fluid. The gallbladder is lodged in the fossa of the inferior surface of the right lobe of the liver. The position of the gallbladder varies with body habitus. Location of the gallbladder is in the right upper quadrant, anterior to the coronal plane.

Fluoroscopic viewing and recording is accomplished with the patient in the erect position. In spot filming of the gallbladder, the patient is in the erect right posterior oblique position using inspiration techniques to move the gallbladder away from superimposed rib structures. The anterior-posterior position of the gallbladder is best viewed using a compression device. The right lateral position will move the gallbladder away from the spine and possible bowel contents. The compression device can also be used to remove bowel gas away from the gallbladder.

Terminal Ileum Fluoroscopy

Fluoroscopic viewing and recording of the ileocecal valve is performed by administering a barium sulfate preparation. Fluoroscopic spot films may be made of any segment of the small bowel as the loops become opacified. When the barium has reached the ileocecal region, fluoroscopy may be performed and compression spot films obtained.

The patient is positioned in the prone position with the compression device overlying the anatomy. Recorded images are accomplished by using either a spot-film camera (105mm) or film/screen spot-film device. When a film/screen cassette is employed, it is advisable to program for four-on-one spot-film images.

Knee Arthrography

Fluoroscopic contrast knee arthrography requires the use of a stress device. The knee is placed in the frame/device to widen or "open up" the side of the knee joint under investigation. This will also enable better distribution of the contrast media around the meniscus. If a stress device is not available, the knee can be manually stressed for the same effect.

Single Contrast Knee Arthrogram

The patient is positioned prone, and each side of the knee joint is fluoroscopically localized. Marking the patient's skin with a dark pen will ensure accurate centering for the closely collimated radiographic views. The anatomic part to be visualized is the posterior aspect of both medial and lateral epicondyles of the femur and tibia. Fluoroscopic views are recorded by a spot-film camera or screen/film spot-film device of each anterior projection and 20° right and left oblique projections.

Double Contrast Knee Arthrogram

The injection of both iodinated contrast media and air is used to better visualize the meniscus.

© GR/St. Lucie Press

1. **Medial meniscus.** Fluoroscopic views are taken with the patient in the supine position on the table. The joint space is manually stressed or by using a stress device to widen the joint space. The patient's leg is rotated to the prone position, and the leg is turned 30° for each fluoroscopic view.

2. **Lateral meniscus.** Fluoroscopic views are taken with the patient in the supine position on the table. The joint space is manually stressed or the stress device is used to widen the knee joint. The patient's leg is rotated to the prone position with the leg rotated 30° for each fluoroscopic view.

Review Questions

1. If 4 gm of tissue absorb 400 ergs of x-rays, what is the absorbed dose?

2. If at 1 ft from the radiation source the intensity of exposure is 480 mR/hr. and you remain at this location for 5 min., you will receive an exposure of 10 mR. What would be your exposure if you moved 2 ft away and remained there for 20 min.?

3. What is the patient's skin dose rate using a 35mm cineradiographic camera at 10 frames/sec. for 1 min.?

4. If the fluoroscopic unit puts out 5 R/hr., how many mR will the fluoroscopist receive in 6 min.?

5. If the fluoroscopic unit is set at 2 mA of tube current, the intensity rate is 250 mR. What is it at 3 mA?

6. What is the patient's skin dose rate using a 35mm cineradiographic camera at 60 frames/sec. for 5 min.?

7. If the fluoroscopic tube puts out 2 R for 15 min., what is the intensity for 12 min.?

Answers to the review questions are on page 180. If you answered 5 or more items correctly, go to the next chapter. If you answered fewer than 5 items correctly, reread the chapter and retake the review questions.

Chapter 16

Fluoroscopy Quality Assurance and Quality Control Program

Objectives

Upon completion of Chapter 16, the reader will be able to:

1. Recognize the responsibilities of the supervisor in maintaining a quality assurance program.
2. Identify the various types of fluoroscopic quality assurance tests.
3. Interpret acceptance testing.
4. Evaluate the x-ray tube and image intensification system, including the closed circuit television system.
5. Recall quality control tests that are performed daily and/or semi-annually.
6. Perform quality control tests on the various fluoroscopic imaging equipment, including the image intensifier and television system.

© GR/St. Lucie Press

Principles of a Quality Assurance Program

In the application of a quality assurance management program to a diagnostic radiology facility, each radiographer is responsible for ensuring that the equipment which they are using is performing in a consistent and satisfactory manner. To fulfill this responsibility, the radiographer needs straightforward and rapid techniques to confirm that the equipment is functioning in a satisfactory and reproducible manner. By using these techniques according to a prescribed schedule and by comparing the resulting data to those collected during acceptance testing of the equipment, the radiographer can affirm that the equipment is satisfactory. Each test should be related to a tolerance range of satisfactory results, with test data falling outside the tolerance range interpreted as indicative of unsatisfactory performance of the equipment. However, before this interpretation is documented, tests yielding unsatisfactory results should be repeated to verify that a problem exists. Data from tests on previous days should be consulted to determine if a trend towards unsatisfactory performance is detectable. Accurate and complete record keeping of quality control test results is essential.

If testing results indicate that the equipment operation is unsatisfactory, the supervisor of the quality control program should be informed so that corrective measures may be implemented. In response to this information, the supervisor should initiate immediate corrective action by arranging for service of the equipment to restore it to satisfactory operation. Prior to clinical use of the serviced equipment, the quality control tests should be repeated to confirm that the equipment has been restored to a satisfactory level of performance.

Quality Assurance Program for Fluoroscopic Systems and Associated Equipment

In any fluoroscopic system, a number of variables can affect the availability of diagnostic information in the image and the exposure of the patient to radiation. Each of these variables should be monitored periodically if a quality assurance program is to be maximally effective in improving image quality and reducing the exposure of the patient to radiation. Results of these monitoring procedures should fall within acceptable tolerance limits of baseline data established when the unit was accepted for clinical use and otherwise judged to be operating properly. In the establishment of acceptable tolerance limits, judgments are required in the level of performance that can reasonably be expected for mass-produced components of x-ray equipment (i.e., test variables that can be tolerated for the components without adverse effects on the clarity of diagnostic information). For each test parameter described, judgments have been made in establishing tolerance limits for test results.

The radiation exposure of a patient undergoing fluoroscopy is strongly dependent on the distance from the x-ray tube to the table supporting the patient. The radiation exposure to the patient will increase with reduced tube-to-table-top distance. Consequently, fluoroscopic systems should provide a minimum tube-to-table-top distance of 12 in., preferably 18 in. To confirm that these distances are provided in a fluoroscopic unit, a special test tool and triangulation geometry are employed.

In a fluoroscopic unit, a radiation beam that extends beyond the image receptor results in excessive scattered radiation reaching the image, increased exposure of the patient to radiation, and a hazardous situation for the fluoroscopist and attending personnel. To alleviate this problem, means should be provided in the fluoroscopic unit to prevent the x-ray beam from extending beyond the image receptor. In any examination, the radiation beam should be confined to the anatomical region of interest. The x-ray beam shutters should provide this confinement by functioning smoothly and uniformly and should close to zero field size. To assess the proper functioning and maximum opening of the fluoroscopic beam restriction system, a special fluoroscopic x-ray beam alignment and restriction test tool is used.

In any fluoroscopic x-ray system, the visibility of anatomic detail in the image is strongly dependent on the electron focusing properties of the image intensifier and its resulting ability to provide high-resolution images. A decrease in the resolving capabilities of the image intensifier leads immediately to loss of diagnostic information in the image. Therefore, the resolution of the image intensifier and fluoroscopic viewing and recording systems should be evaluated periodically. For this evaluation, an image intensifier resolution test pattern is used.

Frequently, patient diagnoses are made from perception in the fluoroscopic image of small low-contrast structures in the patient's anatomy. To ensure the accuracy of these diagnoses, the image intensification fluoroscopic unit must be capable of revealing these low-contrast structures in the image. To test the low-contrast perceptibility performance of the fluoroscopic imaging system, a low-contrast perceptibility phantom is employed.

Alignment of the antiscatter grid with the fluoroscopic x-ray tube and image intensifier is essential to prevent grid cutoff that is reflected in a reduced and non-uniform image brightness. This may obscure needed diagnostic information. To test a fluoroscopic x-ray system for grid alignment, a radiopaque marker is centered on the grid, and its alignment in the fluoroscopic image is examined.

In many fluoroscopic x-ray systems, the exposure rate for a particular examination is established by an automatic brightness control unit to provide an image of adequate brightness on the output screen of the intensifier and on the viewing screen of the television monitor.

It is important to measure the exposure rate periodically under a variety of conditions to ensure that excessive exposure rates are not being produced from a malfunction in the system. These measurements should be evaluated according to established guidelines to verify that the fluoroscopic system is functioning satisfactorily and that excessive exposure rates are not being produced. To obtain the measurements, an appropriate ionization chamber and electrometer are employed.

With any fluoroscopic x-ray beam, filtration should be present, to remove low-energy photons selectively. Filtration will eliminate low-energy photons that are not absorbed by the patient to produce excessive patient radiation dose. The presence of adequate filtration can be verified by measuring beam quality. Test tools for this measurement include an ionization chamber, electrometer, and aluminum attenuators of various thicknesses.

Many fluoroscopic x-ray units are equipped with an automatic exposure control device (phototimer) for automatic timing of exposure during film recording of the fluoroscopic image. A malfunction of the automatic exposure control device produces overexposed or underexposed radiographs, which results in an increase in examination repeat rate and exposure of patients to unnecessary radiation. To evaluate a fluoroscopic automatic exposure control system, an aluminum phantom and digital x-ray timer are used.

Quality assurance (QA) and quality control (QC) are management tools that include policies and procedures designed to optimize the performance of x-ray facility personnel, as well as radiographic and ancillary equipment operation. QA includes the following:

1. QC of radiographic and ancillary equipment.

2. Administration.

3. Education of personnel.

4. Preventive maintenance methods.

Standardized QC tests carried out with care at prescribed intervals are designed to detect slowly evolving, functional x-ray and ancillary equipment abnormalities and to permit corrective action *before* significant deterioration of image quality occurs. The major reason for a QA program is to optimize diagnosis and, therefore, the benefits obtained. A QA program warrants the following expenditures:

1. Personnel costs: QA duties include not only performance of QC tests but also initial eduction and training.
2. Test equipment: QC test equipment cost is relatively small in comparison with the total capital outlay of a radiology department.
3. Decrease in patient flow from testing: QC tests should be performed outside of regular working hours, if possible.

The primary cost saving of a QA program is the result of a decrease in repeat studies that will avoid unnecessary radiation dose to the patient. The cost savings include the following:

1. Wear and tear of the equipment.
2. Decreased down time of equipment.
3. X-ray personnel time.
4. Improvement in patient flow.
5. Decreased cost of equipment service.

Responsibility of Supervisor

The supervisor of each facility in which fluoroscopy x-ray procedures are performed shall establish and maintain a QA and QC program. The supervisor is responsible for assuring that the fluoroscopy and ancillary equipment under his/her authority has been inspected and that QC tests have been performed by a qualified individual. Any individual who is performing QC tests should have special training and continuing education in diagnostic x-ray physics, including **QA** management and **QC** testing.

Quality Assurance Manual

Each fluoroscopy facility shall have a **QA** manual. The **QA** manual shall include a list of names and qualifications of individuals responsible for supervision of **QA**, performance of **QC** tests, and repair or servicing of fluoroscopic and ancillary equipment.

Records for QA Test Equipment

The following **QC** tests shall be performed after repair and/or replacement of any component of the fluoroscopy x-ray system and prior to using the equipment on human beings, if such repair and/or replacement affects the following:

Automatic fluoroscopic collimation

Automatic brightness control (ABC)

Automatic gain control (AGC) system and TV performance

High- and low-level contrast resolution

Phototimer reproducibility

Exposure timer accuracy

Milliampere-seconds linearity

Kilovoltage peak accuracy

Radiation dose rates

Focal spot size

Half value layer

Acceptance testing and physicist's consultation

The consulting physicist should assist the supervisor in the development of the Fluoroscopic Procedure and

Quality Control Manual. The consulting physicist should assist the facility in establishing the protocol for fluoroscopic and ancillary equipment monitoring. This should include all of the following:

1. Establishing the house phantom. The specific phantom to be used for monitoring should be a 6–10 in. of water in a plastic container or equivalent lucite phantom or 1.5 in. of aluminum block measuring 6 × 6 in.
2. Establishing an acceptable penetrometer.
3. Developing consistent machine setup for monitoring beam size, image intensifier position, control panel setting, and other required parameters.
4. Developing the long form for entry of measured data.
5. Entering baseline data to which weekly readings must be compared.
6. Establishing a means to recognize a 25% increase in output rate over calibrated output rate.
7. Providing a means to test for exceeding the 5 Rad/ min. ceiling, if the calibrated output rate is >4 Rad/ min.
8. Indicating what procedures have to be followed in the event either of the two preceding tests are positive.

Acceptance Testing

Complete machine performance tests must include the following items required by the Regulations:

1. Checking the diagnostic x-ray tube housing.
2. Verifying a target-to-panel (table top) distance of at least 12 in. for under-the-table x-ray tubes.
3. Confirming for overhead x-ray tubes a target-to-skin distance of at least 12 in.

Chapter 16 ▪ Fluoroscopy Quality Assurance and Quality Control Program

4. Checking for adequate filtration.

5. Determining primary barrier protection efficiency.

6. Making sure collimators provide protection equal to the diagnostic tube housing.

7. Evaluating collimator beam size.

8. Automatic tracking of beam size linked to image-intensified distance from the table top.

9. Centering the collimator blade to the primary beam.

10. Confirming barrier link interlocks.

11. Checking the five-minute cumulative timer.

12. Measuring and recording of the panel dose rate and the mA and the kVp factors that produce it.

13. Measuring and recording of the maximum achievable output rate and the factors that produce it.

14. Checking of protective barriers.

15. Measuring high-contrast and low-contrast resolution for each television monitor during the acceptance testing procedure.

16. Taking scatter measurements that indicate individual measurements at distances clearly marked and/or an environmental survey of the room indicating iso-exposure curves or profiles for procedures commonly used with a particular unit, taking into consideration where operators and other essential personnel will be placed during a given procedure. The results of measurements must be conspicuously posted on the equipment or in the room.

17. Evaluating Automatic Brightness Control (ABC) and Automatic Gain Control (AGC) systems for invasive and non-invasive tasks. Determining image intensifier gain and conversion gain.

18. Verifying focal spot size, x-ray output waveform, relative conversion, and television performance and video signal.

Establishment of ALARA (As Low As Reasonably Achievable)

The consulting physicist should explain the following regarding the establishment of ALARA:

1. A 5 Rad/min. (1.3 mCkg^{-1}/min.) ceiling does not imply that such a high rate is either desirable or recommended.
2. Every effort should be made to keep radiation exposures as low as is reasonably achievable.
3. The consulting physicist should determine the lowest output rate consistent with an adequate diagnostic-quality image and use that rate as the benchmark to which weekly monitored values are compared.

Fluoroscopy Equipment Quality Control Tests and Frequency

X-ray Tube and Image Intensifier System—Daily

1. **Brightness/contrast optimization of television monitor.** Adjust all TV monitors to show as many steps on the penetrometer as possible. This test should be done before the first fluoroscopic procedure of the day.

2. **Verification, by observation, of the following protective devices:**

   a. Lead curtains
   b. Lead panel
   c. Bucky slot cover

Verify that these protective devices are located in their proper places and/or are working properly.

3. **Fluoroscopic tower locks observation barrier link interlock.** Manual operation of the locks to ascertain/ensure that the fluoroscopic tower locks are functioning properly and that the fluoroscopy power does not drift when positioned. Interlocks should provide protection from accidental exposure to operators when a barrier is not in place or not centered to the primary beam.

4. **Compression device/spoon observation.** Observation and manual operation of the compression device/spoon to ascertain/ensure that the compression device moves in and out easily and is not damaged or splattered with contrast material.

5. **Automatic fluoroscopic phantom collimation.** With a phantom in the x-ray beam, check shutters to assure that they are visible inside the edges of the fluoroscopic image with the tower in the lowest and highest source-to-image distance (SID) positions.

   a. When shutters are fully open, a shutter tangent must be seen at all edges of the monitor.

   b. In the "auto shutter" mode, the size of the field seen on the monitor should not change, regardless of whether the image intensifier is close to the table or at its maximum condition.

6. **Low-contrast performance test.**
   Test tool: Phantom, aluminum sheet containing 1- to 7-mm holes or two 2-cm aluminum plates containing 1- to 7-mm holes. Determine the reproducibility of low-contrast performance by comparing the current to previous (baseline) image.

7. **Kilovoltage (kVp) and milliamperage (mA) monitoring test.**

Test tool: Phantom (low-contrast test object). Under specific standard measuring conditions, monitor fluoroscopic kVp and mA during any procedure that will result in an average patient control setting. The readings should be entered in a log and compared to a reading taken at the time of calibration and evaluation for:

a. Compliance with <25% increase in output rate.

b. Compliance with the requirement not to exceed an output rate of 5 Rad/min. if calibrated output rate was >4 Rad/min.

c. Changes that must be reported to the responsible individual for immediate correction.

8. **Mobile spacer for C-arm fluoroscopes/observation.** Ascertain that spacer frame or cones which provide for a source-to-skin distance of not less than 12 in. are permanently attached so that their removal would require tools.

X-ray Tube and Image Intensifier System—Semi-Annually

1. **Shutters test.**
   Test tools: Phantom, cardboard film holder. When shutters are fully open, a shutter tangent must be seen at all edges of the monitor. In "auto shutter" mode the size of the field seen on the monitor should not change appreciably regardless of whether the image intensifier is close to the table top or as far away as possible.

   The maximum fluoroscopic beam size must not exceed the size of the image intensifier.

2. **Automatic Brightness Control (ABC) tracking test.**
   Test tools: Dosimeter, homogeneous phantom, aluminum sheets, lead blocker, acrylic sheets, ion

Chapter 16 ■ Fluoroscopy Quality Assurance and Quality Control Program

chamber. Ascertain that the ABC responds to variations in simulated changes in tissue densities. Take readings of kVp and mA with only 50% thickness of house phantom in the beam, place the entire phantom in the beam, and then add more attenuating material in the beam. The readings should be proportional to the amount of material placed in the beam.

3. **Gain control system test.**
   Test tools: Dosimeter and homogeneous patient-equivalent phantom. Either the Automatic Brightness Control (ABC) or the Automatic Exposure Control (AEC) is used on most fluoroscopic imaging systems to control technical factors—kVp and mA or pulse width—to ensure that radiation sufficient to form an adequate image reaches the image intensifier. Many fluoroscopic systems are also equipped with an Automatic Gain Control (AGC), which rapidly varies the gain of the video system to maintain a bright image on the video display/TV monitor. A high-quality AGC system should be able to compensate for at least an additional 7.5 cm of acrylic on top of the standard 15-cm phantom.

4. **High-contrast resolution test.**
   Test tools: Phantom or scattering material, resolution test pattern (copper mesh) or a relatively thick (0.05 to 0.10 mm) lead resolution pattern at a relatively low kVp (50 to 60), penetrometer. Determine the unit's ability to reproduce thin lines and spaces, which are practically black lines and white spaces in the image.

   NOTE: Resolution patterns with a maximum frequency of 5 cycles/mm (c/mm) are adequate. If copper mesh patterns are used, the pattern should contain at least 15 to 20 mesh/cam for fluoroscopic systems and at least 25 mesh/cam for cine and PFS film devices.

© GR/St. Lucie Press

5. **Low-contrast resolution test.**
Test tools: Rest pattern, such as a thin (0.01 to 0.02 mm) lead resolution pattern with some additional scattering material or with a penetrometer consisting of two 2-cm aluminum plates and containing holes ranging in size from 1 to 7 mm, penetrometer, aluminum wafer containing a series of holes placed between two aluminum plates. Determine the unit's ability to resolve relatively large objects that differ slightly in radiopacity from the surrounding area(s). Look for the smallest diameter hole pairs discernible.

NOTE: Resolution patterns with a maximum frequency of 5 cycles/mm (c/mm) are adequate. If a copper mesh pattern is used, the pattern should contain at least 15 to 20 mesh/cam for fluoroscopic systems and at least 25 mesh/cam for cine and PFS film devices.

Resolution should be measured for each television monitor separately.

6. **Five-minute timer test.**
Test tools: Stopwatch, homogeneous phantom. The cumulative timer should sound an audible alarm at the end of a pre-set time interval.

CAUTION: Use precautions against damaging the image intensifier by placing an attenuator such as a phantom in the beam or, if possible, closing the shutters completely.

7. **Actual fluoroscopic beam size test.**
Test tools: Alignment template or nine pennies and tape measure. Automatic beam limitation and accuracy of X-Y scales should be ±3% of source-to-image distance.

8. **Filtration (HVL measurement) test.**
Test tools: 100 aluminum sheets, dosimeter/ion chamber, semi-log paper. Determine the amount of

aluminum equivalent filtration in the x-ray beam for various kilovoltages used. The unit is in compliance if the HVL is not less than the value specified in Table 2 of Title 17, Chapter 5, Subchapter 4, Section 30308 (a)(3).

9. **Minimum source-to-table-top distance.**
Test tools: Tape measure, spot film, radiopaque spacers. Determine by congruent triangles the actual distance from the source to the top of the table.

10. **Kilovoltage accuracy.**
Test tools: kVp cassette or direct reading, noninvasive kVp device. The physicist should ascertain that measured kVp matches indicated value with a tolerance of ±5%. The actual vs. indicated kVp shall be maintained as specified by the x-ray equipment manufacturer ±5%, with less over a limited range (e.g., ±2 kVp to 60–100 kVp).

11. **Typical patient exposure rates.**
Test tools: Dosimeter/ion chamber capable of measuring the exposure rate, homogeneous patient-equivalent phantom that is 9 in. of water, 7 $7/_8$ in. of lucite, 21 cm, 15 cm, 6 cm of acrylic, or 3 mm of aluminum. Determine the fluoroscopic exposure rate with the unit for the typical patient under conditions specified in the Regulations to optimize contrast and minimize patient exposure. The exposure rate is affected by age, design, kVp, and filtration (2–3 mR/min., 6-in. mode with grid: 1.5–2.5 mR/min., 9-in. mode without grid). Maximum AEC should be set at 80–90 kVp. The exposure for a single room should be constant.

Most fluoroscopy systems should be able to produce adequate images with entrance exposures of 2–3 R/min. in the 15-cm mode. Differences in exposure rates exceeding ±25% between rooms should be investigated. For systems operating with a grid in place, the exposure rates will be 1.5 to 2 times higher.

© GR/St. Lucie Press

Principles of Fluoroscopic Image Intensification and Television Systems: Workbook and Laboratory Manual

12. **Maximum exposure rates.**
    Test tools: Dosimeter/ion chamber, lead sheets, aluminum attenuators. Determine the highest possible exposure rate(s) the unit can deliver to the patient.

13. **Apron/glove integrity.**
    Test tools: X-ray film. Determine that protective devices do not have voids or cracks that would compromise protection desired.

    NOTE: **Resolution** can be affected by focal spot, imaging geometry, the quality and focus of the optical system, image intensifier, video camera, and television monitor, and, for conventional spot films, screen film contact.

    Distortion (pincushion or barrel) or stretching the image can be caused by the image intensifier tube, optics, video camera and circuitry, or the television monitor. For distortion measurements, a coarse copper mesh, such as screen film contact mesh or a copper mesh with 7 mm spacing between the wires, can be used. It is difficult to quantify the amount of acceptable distortion. Distortion should be vertically and horizontally symmetrical and should appear the same for fluoroscopic, cine, and photofluorospot film images.

Fluoroscopy Imaging Equipment Quality Control Tests: Test Frequency

1. **Image lag.**
   Test tools: Lag shutter, storage oscilloscope and camera. Lag is a phenomenon associated with video imaging systems. Lag degrades the quality of the fluoroscopic image and is defined as the percent video signal remaining in the third video field after light is removed from the photocathode. Vidicon exhibits more lag than plumbicon. The TV monitor should be

set up using a commercially available video signal generator.

2. **MaS linearity.**
Test tools: Ion chamber or digital timer. The average ratios of exposure to the indicated milliampere/sec. product (mR/mAs) obtained at any two consecutive tube current settings shall not differ by more than 0.10 times their sum.

3. **Exposure reproducibility.**
Test tool: Dosimeter. The coefficient of variation should not exceed ±5%.

4. **Phototimers.**
Test tools: Dosimeter, lead sheets, homogeneous phantom. The coefficient of variation should not exceed ±10% in exposure.

5. **Spot-film and film camera exposures.**
Test tools: Dosimeter, homogeneous phantom (13–50 $nCkg^{-1}$/frame intensifier for 9-in. mode; approximately 7 $nCkg^{-1}$/frame at intensifier for 6-in. mode). High-quality, relatively low-noise images are needed for cardiac diagnosis. Large number of frames/sec., 30–60 in about 10 sec. for each view or injection. Patient entrance exposures range from 50 to 150 Rads or more.

NOTE: There is general agreement that approximately 15 microRoentgens/frame is required at the entrance to the image intensifier for adequate cine studies using the 23-cam mode.

■ Principles of Fluoroscopic Image Intensification and Television Systems: Workbook and Laboratory Manual

Review Questions

1. Specific phantoms to be used for quality control testing are
   a. 3 in. of lucite.
   b. 10 in. of plastic.
   c. 1.5 in. of aluminum block.
   d. 24 in. of water.

2. Complete machine performance testing must include the following, *except*
   a. diagnostic x-ray tube housing.
   b. processor chemistry.
   c. filtration.
   d. Automatic Brightness Control.

3. Quality control tests to determine x-ray tube potential and current should be completed
   a. daily.
   b. weekly.
   c. semi-annually.
   d. yearly.

4. The following test tools are used to measure maximum x-ray tube exposure rate:

   _____   _____

   _____

5. Which type of test tool is used to measure pincushion distortion?
   a. dosimeter
   b. course copper mesh
   c. ion chamber
   d. $7\,^7/_8$ in. of lucite

6. Which type of television pick-up tube exhibits more lag?

Answers to the review questions are on page 180. If you answered 5 or more items correctly, take the review test on page 183. If you answered fewer than 5 items correctly, reread the chapter and retake the review questions.

176

© GR/St. Lucie Press

Appendix A

Answer Key to Review Questions

CHAPTER ONE

1. input phosphor and photocathode
   electrostatic lens
   accelerating anode
   output phosphor
2. CeI
3. c
4. cathode
5. electrostatic lens
6. d
7. subjective lens
8. conversion factor
9. b
10. flux, minification
11. 144 times
12. a,b,c
13. 3,000
14. a,b,c,d
15. b
16. output phosphor
17. farther
18. vignetting
19. a
20. increase
21. a
22. b
23. b
24. d
25. 2.25 times

CHAPTER TWO

1. b
2. focal point
3. relative aperture
4. quadruple
5. a
6. 600 mR/hr.

© GR/St. Lucie Press

CHAPTER THREE

1. 525
2. b
3. video
4. $1/30$
5. interlaced scanning
6. glass faceplate

   signal plate

   target
7. a
8. b
9. 30
10. bandpass, bandwidth
11. 50
12. d
13. 8
14. 525
15. b

CHAPTER FOUR

1. d
2. d
3. the exposure is synchronous with the open time of the camera shutter
4. 0.001
5. magnetic field
6. at least once each year, following alterations of the image assembly and the power source
7. it takes a certain amount of time for the image to build up and decay on the vidicon camera tube
8. 3,600 mR/min. or 3.6 R/min.

9. synchronization, frame rate, f/number of the optical system
10. c

CHAPTER FIVE

1. b
2. c
3. d
4. a
5. a

CHAPTER SIX

1. stray, leakage
2. ionizing
3. radicals
4. radiant, x-ray
5. short, long
6. amplitude
7. mA
8. tube
9. kVp
10. inner
11. valence

CHAPTER SEVEN

1. stray, scatter
2. dead man
3. b
4. b
5. 12.5 mR
6. 18
7. 2.5 mm

8. 5 R/min.
9. once each week
10. 30
11. 2,000 mR

CHAPTER EIGHT

1. a
2. c
3. b
4. c
5. 30
6. cessation of sperm

CHAPTER NINE

1. 25
2. long-term
3. undifferentiated, rapidly dividing, active proliferation
4. mA, kVp, collimation
5. x-ray examination rate, mean gonadal dose per exam, function of future children
6. 1 Rad

CHAPTER TEN

1. b
2. patient
3. 50 mR/hr.
4. 135
5. absorbed
6. 2.5
7. 100 mR/hr.
8. 0.25 mm Pb

9. once each week
10. b
11. carbon fiber

CHAPTER ELEVEN

1. 5 Rem
2. month
3. 100 mR
4. inexpensive

 gives an estimate of the integrated dose

 provides a permanent record

 provides an objective review and detects problems
5. no permanent record

 frequent reading, tabulation, and recharging

 may be accidentally discharged

 limited measurement
6. 100 mR
7. 20 mR

CHAPTER TWELVE

1. 0.5 mm
2. mitotic activity
3. d
4. 1 Rad
5. 6.25 R
6. b

CHAPTER THIRTEEN

1. 525
2. 25 sec.

© GR/St. Lucie Press

3. 196 times
4. apron, gloves, eye, thyroid shields
5. 2.2 R/min.

CHAPTER FOURTEEN

1. bandpass
2. time, distance, shielding
3. 97
4. visual acuity
5. 12–15
6. a

CHAPTER FIFTEEN

1. 1 Rad
2. 10 mR
3. 1,200 mR/min. or 1.2 R/min.

4. 0.5 R or 500 mR
5. $\dfrac{250 \text{ mR}}{2 \text{ mA}}$ = 125 mR/mA × 3 mA = 375 mR
6. 36,000 mR or 36.0 R
7. $\dfrac{2 \text{ R}}{15 \text{ mA}}$ = 0.13 R/mA × 12 mA = 1.6 R

CHAPTER SIXTEEN

1. c
2. b
3. b
4. dosimeter/ion chamber
   lead sheets
   aluminum attenuators
5. b
6. vidicon

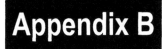

Statement of Competency Technologist's Use of Fluoroscopy Equipment

I, _____, holder of
　　　　(Please Print Physician Name)
[ ]　Radiology Supervisor and Operator Certificate
[ ]　Fluoroscopy Supervisor and Operator Certificate
　　　Certificate number_____, expiration date_____, do hereby
attest that _____, C.R.T. has successfully completed
　　　　　(Print Technologist's Name)
supervised competency-based clinical education and training given from_____
through _____, at _____ in the
　　　　　　　　　　　(Name and Address of clinical facility)
following areas and procedures:

[ ] Gastrointestinal tract
_____
_____

[ ] Vascular and Angio Systems
_____
_____

[ ] Orthopedic Procedures
_____
_____

[ ] Other (Please specify)
_____
_____

Signature of Doctor who supervised or offered clinical training:
_____ Date signed _____
Business telephone number (___) _____ x _____

© GR/St. Lucie Press

Appendix C

Review Test

DIRECTIONS: Choose the best answer that completes the statement or answers the question.

1. The major reason that image intensified fluoroscopy is employed is that it allows for
   a. dynamic viewing.
   b. rapid development.
   c. high visual acuity.
   d. low patient exposure.

2. Portable intensified fluoroscopy used for diagnostic purposes must not exceed ____ at the table top.
   a. 1 R/min.
   b. 3 R/min.
   c. 5 R/min.
   d. 10 R/min.

3. Which type of vision is most commonly employed during conventional fluoroscopic exams?
   a. photopic
   b. scoptopic
   c. mesopic
   d. fovotopic

4. As the illumination of the light source increases, visual acuity
   a. increases.
   b. decreases.
   c. remains the same.

5. The time over which the human eye can store a visual image is termed ____ time.
   a. adaptation
   b. acuity
   c. integration
   d. illumination

6. Which of the following structures is first to intercept light incident on the eye?
   a. rods
   b. iris
   c. cornea
   d. cones

7. The normal view distance for binocular vision is
   a. 1–2 in.
   b. 4–8 in.
   c. 12–5 in.
   d. 16–20 in.

8. In general, during conventional fluoroscopic examinations the preferred technique is
   a. high kVp, low mA.
   b. high kVp, low mAs.
   c. low kVp, high mAs.
   d. low kVp, high mA.

9. Which of the following properties are associated with cones rather than rods?
   a. contrast perception
   b. color detection
   c. visual acuity
   d. all of the above

© GR/St. Lucie Press

■ Principles of Fluoroscopic Image Intensification and Television Systems: Workbook and Laboratory Manual

10. How long does it take for the fluoroscopic table to move from the horizontal to the vertical position?
   a. 5–15 sec.
   b. 10–20 sec.
   c. 25–30 sec.
   d. 30–40 sec.

11. Visible light
   a. is not part of the electromagnetic spectrum.
   b. has higher energy than x-rays.
   c. is the only part of the electromagnetic spectrum we can see.
   d. has lower energy than radio waves.

12. Most modern image intensifiers use an input fluorescent screen layer that is composed of
   a. calcium tungstate.
   b. cesium iodide.
   c. barium lead sulfate.
   d. zinc cadmium sulfide.

13. The conversion of light energy into a proportional amount of electrons is accomplished by a/an
   a. electron gun.
   b. photomultiplier.
   c. electrostatic lens.
   d. photocathode.

14. The acceleration of the electron stream inside the image intensifier requires a potential difference (voltage) of
   a. 25 volts.
   b. 50 volts.

   c. 25 kilovolts.
   d. 50 kilovolts.

15. The output screen of an image intensifier functions to convert ____ into ___.
   a. light, electrons
   b. light, x-rays
   c. electrons, light
   d. x-rays, electrons

16. The target-to-panel and target-to-skin distance shall not be less than
   a. 18 in.
   b. 35 cm.
   c. 40 in.
   d. 12 in.

17. The squared ratio of input screen to output screen size is called
   a. minification ratio.
   b. flux gain.
   c. magnification ratio.
   d. conversion ratio.

18. A 9-in. input screen and a 1-in. output screen increases brightness
   a. 9 times.
   b. 18 times.
   c. 40 times.
   d. 81 times.

19. The point in the image intensifier tube where the electrons cross over is termed the
   a. optical point.
   b. electronic focal point.
   c. input focal point.
   d. output focal point.

20. In order to prevent light from scattering back to the photocathode

184

© GR/St. Lucie Press

layer of the image intensifier, a thin sheet of aluminum is placed onto the

   a. input phosphor.

   b. photocathode.

   c. output phosphor.

   d. output focal spot.

21. Which of the following could be used to increase brightness gain?

   a. a higher x-ray beam intensity

   b. decrease minification ratio

   c. increase accelerating voltage

   d. all of the above

22. The focusing of the electron stream in the image intensifier tube is accomplished by placing a ____ charge on the electrostatic lens.

   a. negative

   b. positive

   c. neither of the above

23. Distortion which occurs with an image intensifier tube that demonstrates a dimmer density image at the periphery is called

   a. interlacing.

   b. vignetting.

   c. diminution.

   d. edge spread function.

24. The random pattern of scattered radiation, which often results in an image intensifier tube that has the appearance of "snow" or "crawling ants," is

   a. lens opacity.

   b. vignetting.

   c. quantum noise.

   d. flicker effect.

25. The ratio of the luminance in candelas of the output phosphor to the input exposure rate in milliroentgens/sec. defines

   a. brightness gain.

   b. flux gain.

   c. minification ratio.

   d. conversion factor.

26. The output phosphor of most modern image intensifiers is

   a. zinc cadmium sulfide.

   b. cesium iodide.

   c. sodium iodide.

   d. calcium tungstate.

27. The output phosphor converts electrons into

   a. secondary electrons.

   b. light photons.

   c. x-ray photons.

   d. globules.

28. The radiation exposure rate at the output phosphor will increase with increased

   a. x-ray collimation.

   b. x-ray tube current.

   c. x-ray tube rotation.

   d. filtration.

29. Proper collimation of the fluoroscopic x-ray beam will

   a. decrease patient exposure.

   b. reduce scatter radiation.

   c. improve image quality.

   d. all of the above.

30. For fluoroscopic equipment with automatic exposure rate control, the x-ray tube current and potential shall be monitored at least

■ Principles of Fluoroscopic Image Intensification and Television Systems: Workbook and Laboratory Manual

a. once each day.

b. once each week.

c. once each year.

d. once every three years.

31. Statistical fluctuations in the radiographic image which result in a grainy appearance is called

a. contrast.

b. quantum mottle.

c. sievert.

d. resolution.

32. The resolution of cesium iodide image tubes is approximately

a. 4 lp/mm.

b. 1 lp/mm.

c. 10 lp/mm.

d. 20 lp/mm.

33. Which of the following cannot reduce patient exposure and operator exposure?

a. restricting the x-ray beam "on" time to a minimum

b. using the lowest mA and highest kVp

c. restricting the x-ray beam to the smallest size

d. keeping patient-screen distance to a maximum

34. A photocell located between the image intensifier and the television camera system that is designed to maintain a range of brightness is a

a. photoemitter.

b. vidicon.

c. automatic brightness stabilizer.

d. none of the above.

35. In order to maintain image clarity, the path of electron flow from the photocathode to the output phosphor is controlled by

a. accelerating anode.

b. electrostatic lens.

c. the vacuum glass tube.

d. input phosphor.

36. The image intensifier input phosphor differs from the output phosphor in that the input phosphor

a. is much larger than the output.

b. emits electrons, and the output phosphor emits light photons.

c. absorbs electrons, and the output phosphor absorbs light photons.

d. is a fixed size, and the output phosphor size can vary.

37. The total brightness gain of an image intensifier is a result of (1) flux gain, (2) minification ratio, (3) focusing gain.

a. 1

b. 2

c. 1 and 2

d. 1 and 3

e. 1, 2, and 3

38. The electronic image which is produced at the input side of a television camera is scanned by means of a/an

© GR/St. Lucie Press

a. photo beam.

b. proton gun.

c. electron gun.

d. photocathode.

39. Each frame of a television picture consists of

a. 262 scanning lines.

b. 525 scanning lines.

c. 1,050 scanning lines.

d. 2,200 scanning lines.

40. The input screen of a televisin camera tube converts the light image from the image intensifier into a/an

a. x-ray image.

b. electronic image.

c. visible image.

d. none of the above.

41. The electronic signal which carries the information from the television camera to the monitor is termed the

a. synchronization pulse.

b. bandpass.

c. return beam.

d. video signal.

42. In the television monitor, an electron gun repeats the pattern of the television camera tube's image onto a/an

a. photocathode.

b. fluorescent screen.

c. photographic film.

d. x-ray film.

43. In order to ensure the proper eye integration, a frame must be completed every

a. $1/30$ sec.

b. $1/10$ sec.

c. $1/8$ sec.

d. $1/5$ sec.

44. In order to prevent the flicker effect during viewing of the television image, a technique called____ is used.

a. preamplification

b. interlaced scanning

c. synchronization

d. depolarization

45. Which of the following are television camera tubes?

a. vidicon

b. image orthicon

c. plumbicon

d. all of the above

46. The electron beam in the television camera tube is produced by

a. thermionic emission.

b. photoemission.

c. electroemission.

d. photoconduction.

47. The electron beam in the television camera tube is controlled by the

a. deflecting coils.

b. electrostatic coils.

c. focusing coils.

d. all of the above.

48. The target assembly of a television camera tube consists of

a. window.

b. target.

© GR/St. Lucie Press

Principles of Fluoroscopic Image Intensification and Television Systems: Workbook and Laboratory Manual

c. signal plate.

d. all of the above.

49. Which of the following will send the video signal?

    a. window

    b. target

    c. signal plate

    d. photomultiplier

50. In the optical coupling arrangement, which is nearest the television camera tube?

    a. objective lens

    b. camera lens

    c. beam splitter

    d. mirror

51. When the video signal is modulated, that means its _____ is changing in a controlled fashion.

    a. intensity

    b. frequency

    c. amplitude

    d. all of the above

52. The electron beam of the television camera tube is _____ with the television monitor.

    a. modulated

    b. synchronized

    c. an area beam

    d. blanked

53. One television frame is equal to

    a. 1 television field.

    b. 2 television fields.

    c. $252\,^1/_2$ lines.

    d. 17 milliseconds.

54. The fluoroscopic television operates at a frame rate of

    a. $262\,^1/_2$ frames/sec.

    b. 525 frames/sec.

    c. 30 frames/sec.

    d. 60 frames/sec.

55. Horizontal television resolution is limited principally by the

    a. frame rate.

    b. field rate.

    c. bandpass.

    d. lines per frame.

56. The brightness of the image varies directly as mA and as the 50th power of kVp. Thus, as the kVp would vary from 80 to 88, a 10% change, there could be a ____% change in brightness.

    a. 20

    b. 50

    c. 10

    d. 30

57. In most magnetic tape recorders, the magnetic head gap width is on the order of

    a. 100 mm.

    b. 0.01 mm.

    c. 0.001 mm.

    d. 10 mm.

58. The recording head of the video tape receives a changing electric signal which is transformed into a changing

    a. magnetic field.

    b. electronic pulse.

    c. video signal.

    d. current.

59. For fluoroscopic equipment that has the x-ray tube below the table,

© GR/St. Lucie Press

the exposure rate shall be measured ____ above the table.

a. 1 in.

b. 1 cm

c. 1 ft

d. none of the above

60. The minimum height of the primary barrier is

a. 7 ft.

b. 8 ft.

c. 6.6 ft.

d. 10 ft.

61. Secondary barriers are only necessary for

a. radiographic units

b. combined R/F units

c. tomographic units

d. all of the above

e. none of the above

62. If the x-ray tube is above the table, the exposure rate shall be measure at ____ above the table.

a. 12 in.

b. 18 in.

c. 10 in.

d. 30 in.

63. When automatic exposure rate control is used, the useful beam exposure rate shall be measured with a phantom equivalent to _____ intercepting the useful beam.

a. 12 in. of water

b. 7 $7/8$ in. of water

c. 9 in. of water

d. 12 in. of lucite

64. When the TPD is increased from 12 in. to 18 in., the skin entrance exposure will be reduced by

a. 30%.

b. 60%.

c. 40%.

d. none of the above.

65. Fluoroscopic operators shall restrict the beam "on" time to a minimum. Doubling the exposure time will also ____ the exposure to the patient.

a. quadruple

b. one-half

c. double

d. one-fourth

66. The intensity of the x-ray beam at the table top of a fluoroscope should not exceed ____ for each mA of tube current operating at 80 kVp.

a. 2.2 R/min.

b. 4.9 R/min.

c. 5 R/min.

d. 10 R/min.

67. A certain x-ray tube, at some given kilovoltage peak, delivers 4 milliroentgen per 1 milliampere second at 40 in. of distance. At 1 in. distance, the radiation output from the x-ray beam will be

a. 16 mR/mAs.

b. 8 mR/mAs.

c. 2 mR/mAs.

d. 1 mR/mAs.

68. During fluoroscopic image intensification, the technologist should

■ Principles of Fluoroscopic Image Intensification and Television Systems: Workbook and Laboratory Manual

restrict the x-ray beam to the smallest size practicable. Doubling the exposure field will result in _____ the patient exposure.

a. double

b. one-half

c. one-fourth

d. quadruple

69. The intensity of radiation varies inversely to the square of the distance. As one moves away from the x-ray source, he/she will receive less radiation because

    a. the primary photons are attenuated.

    b. the x-ray beam diverges from its point source.

    c. the primary photons are scattered in opposite directions.

    d. the rotating anode has a tendency to absorb some intensity.

70. Which of the following is directly proportional to the exposure delivered to the patient?

    a. kVp

    b. mA

    c. thickness of the filter

    d. target-to-panel distance

71. If 3 gm of tissue absorb 300 ergs of x-ray energy, what is the dose?

    a. 1 Rad

    b. 3 Rad

    c. 4 Rad

    d. 300 Rad

72. The basic provisions regarding mobile fluoroscopy are as follows:

(1) inherent provisions so that the machine cannot be operated at a skin distance of less than 18 in.; (2) image intensification must be provided; (3) conventional fluoroscopic screens are not permitted; (4) it shall be impossible to operate the fluoroscope when the collimator or diaphragm is not in place.

a. 1, 2, 3

b. 1, 2, 3, 4

c. 2, 3

d. 2, 3, 4

73. Fluoroscopic equipment with an AEC control shall not be operable at any combination of tube potential and current in excess of

a. 5 R/min.

b. 10 R/min.

c. 2.2 R/min.

d. none of the above.

74. The following facts should be given to women employees operating x-ray equipment: (1) the first 3 months of pregnancy are the most important; (2) the actual dose received by the fetus is less than the dose received by the mother; (3) at the present occupational dose equivalent limits, the risk to the unborn baby is considered to be small; (4) there is no need for women to be concerned about sterility or loss of the ability to bear children.

a. 1, 3, 4

b. 2, 4

c. 1, 2, 3, 4

d. 1, 2, 3

© GR/St. Lucie Press

Appendix C ▪ Review Test

75. Fluoroscopic operator exposure to scattered radiation is directly proportional to

    a.   beam intensity.

    b.   output phosphor.

    c.   image brightness.

    d.   patient exposure.

76. Isoexposure contours during fluoroscopy will show that at a distance of 3 ft from the head of the table, the radiographer will receive

    a.   50 mR/hr.

    b.   100 mR/hr.

    c.   1 mR/hr.

    d.   500 mR/hr.

77. Compton scatter is the interaction of

    a.   the incident photon and the valence electron.

    b.   the high-speed electron and the k-shell electron.

    c.   the incident photon and the k-shell electron.

    d.   the scattered photon and the k-shell electron.

78. The following are advantages of using a film badge: (1) inexpensive, (2) reusable, (3) provides a permanent record, (4) can detect problems, (5) provides an objective review.

    a.   1, 2, 3

    b.   1, 2, 4

    c.   2, 3, 4

    d.   1, 3, 4, 5

79. The following are possible disadvantages of a pocket dosimeter: (1) no permanent record, (2) frequent recharging required, (3) subject to accidental discharge, (4) range of measurement limited.

    a.   1, 2

    b.   1

    c.   1, 3, 4

    d.   1, 3

    e.   1, 2, 3, 4

80. When the portable C-arm is used for an anteroposterior chest view, in which direction from the x-ray tube is there the most scattered radiation?

    a.   45° from the primary beam

    b.   90° from the primary beam

    c.   135° from the primary beam

    d.   180° from the primary beam

81. Which method of gonadal shielding is best during fluoroscopy?

    a.   shaped, contact shield

    b.   shadow shielding

    c.   flat contact shielding

    d.   none is needed

82. Increasing fluoroscopic x-ray tube current in mA will (1) provide a brighter image, (2) increase the patient exposure, (3) decrease the operator exposure, (4) increase the radiation exposure rate at the output phosphor.

    a.   1, 2

    b.   1, 2, 3

    c.   1, 2, 4

    d.   1, 2, 3, 4

83. Increasing the peak kilovoltage will (1) increase the penetrating power

© GR/St. Lucie Press

191

of the x-ray beam, (2) reduce the patient skin exposure, (3) decrease the radiation exposure rate at the output phosphor, (4) allow for the use of lower x-ray tube current.

a. 1, 4

b. 1, 2, 3

c. 1, 2, 4

d. 1, 3, 4

e. 1, 2, 3, 4

84. When x-rays are directed toward the patient, most are

a. absorbed by the patient.

b. scattered by the patient.

c. absorbed by the operator.

d. absorbed in air.

85. The dead-man type exposure switch (1) terminates the exposure when pressure is released, (2) operates by circuit closing contact maintained by continuous pressure, (3) circuit will be closed when the operator dies, (4) is an electromagnetic relay contact.

a. 1, 2, 4

b. 1, 2, 3

c. 4

d. 1, 2

e. 1, 3, 4

86. When the optional high-level control is activated, the equipment shall not be operable at any combination of tube current and potential that will result in an exposure rate in excess of

a. 10 R/min.

b. 5 R/min.

c. 2.2 R/min.

d. none of the above.

87. X-ray tube housing must be so constructed that the leakable radiation at a distance of 1 m from the target cannot exceed

a. 100 mR/hr.

b. 100 R/hr.

c. 10 R/hr.

d. 10 mR/hr.

88. The bucky slot cover/protective curtain should have at least _____ equivalent material.

a. 0.25 mm Al

b. 0.50 mm Al

c. 0.25 mm Pb

d. 0.50 mm Pb

89. The mA setting for fluoroscopy is typically less than

a. 5.

b. 100.

c. 10.

d. 500.

90. The operator must monitor the tube current and potential at least

a. once each day.

b. once each week.

c. once each month.

d. every 3 years.

91. Genetic dose refers to the

a. effects of radiation on an irradiated person's gonads.

b. exposure measure by the film badges worn at the gonadal level.

c. effects exhibited in future offspring of persons who have been irradiated.

d. dose that penetrates gonadal shielding.

92. All of the following affect patient exposure *except*

a. 3-phase generators.

b. collimation.

c. target-to-panel distance.

d. exposure time.

93. A high radiation area is any area, accessible to individuals, in which there exists radiation at such levels that an individual could receive in any 1 hr. a dose to the whole body in excess of

a. 5 mRem.

b. 50 mRem.

c. 500 mRem.

d. 100 mRem.

94. The roentgen is a unit of

a. absorbed dose.

b. absorbed dose equivalent.

c. exposure.

d. energy equivalent.

95. The genetically significant dose is a factor of which of the following parameters: (1) x-ray examination rate, (2) mean gonadal dose per examination, (3) number of chromosomes damaged, (4) function of future children.

a. 1, 3, 4

b. 2, 3

c. 1, 2, 4

d. 1, 2, 3

e. 3, 4

96. Radiosensitivity of the body is influenced by all of the following *except*

a. type of radiation and dose rate.

b. size of the cell.

c. total dose the body receives.

d. type of cells being irradiated.

97. All of the following directly influence the table-top exposure rate *except*

a. filtration.

b. kVp.

c. target-to-panel distance.

d. light in the fluoroscopy room.

98. What is the maximum exposure a pregnant occupational worker may receive during the 9 months of gestation?

a. 100 mRem

b. 200 mRem

c. 500 mRem

d. none of the above

99. Which type of table-top material significantly reduces patient exposure?

a. barium fluorochloride

b. carbon fiber

c. chrom-aluminum

d. bakelite

100. If the output intensity is 128 mR/hr. at 12 mA of tube current, what is the intensity at 15 mA?

a. 160 mR/hr.

b. 102.4 mR/hr.

c. 1536 mR/hr.

d. none of the above

© GR/St. Lucie Press

Review Test Answer Key

1.	a	35.	b	68.	a
2.	c	36.	a	69.	b
3.	b	37.	c	70.	b
4.	a	38.	c	71.	a
5.	c	39.	b	72.	d
6.	c	40.	b	73.	b
7.	c	41.	d	74.	c
8.	a	42.	b	75.	d
9.	d	43.	a	76.	a
10.	c	44.	b	77.	a
11.	c	45.	d	78.	d
12.	b	46.	a	79.	e
13.	d	47.	a	80.	c
14.	c	48.	d	81.	a
15.	c	49.	c	82.	c
16.	d	50.	b	83.	c
17.	a	51.	b	84.	a
18.	d	52.	b	85.	d
19.	b	53.	b	86.	b
20.	c	54.	c	87.	a
21.	a	55.	c	88.	c
22.	b	56.	b	89.	a
23.	b	57.	c	90.	b
24.	c	58.	a	91.	c
25.	d	59.	b	92.	a
26.	b	60.	c	93.	d
27.	b	61.	e	94.	c
28.	b	62.	a	95.	c
29.	d	63.	c	96.	b
30.	b	64.	a	97.	d
31.	b	65.	c	98.	c
32.	a	66.	a	99.	b
33.	d	67.	d	100.	a
34.	c				

Appendix D

Laboratory Experiments

The laboratory exercises are designed for use with the fluoroscopic image intensifier, closed circuit television system, and inexpensive, easily available radiation protection and measurement equipment. Each laboratory experiment should require from 1 to 2 hours for completion. The laboratory analysis has been designed to be brief but to the point.

The following materials are recommended for use with the laboratory experiments in this workbook. Depending on the type of fluoroscopic equipment you are performing these experiments on, it may be necessary to substitute alternative materials or equipment, and the arrangement of the experiment may have to be adapted to meet your specific needs. All of these experiments can be performed using routine fluoroscopic equipment normally found in any radiology department. The suggested fluoroscopic exposure factors may also have to be adjusted to the output and availability of your equipment.

Suggested Material for Experiments

1. Ionization chamber-type survey meter (Victoreen Condenser R-meter).
2. Phantom part: chest, abdomen, pelvis, or CT water bottle.

© GR/St. Lucie Press

3. Tape measure or ruler.
4. Protective apparel.
5. Personnel monitoring device.
6. Spot-film device.
7. Screen/film spot-film cassette.
8. Quarter or half-dollar coin.
9. Fluoroscopic resolution test tool.
10. 7 $7/8$-in. lucite phantom or 2-in. aluminum phantometer.
11. Adhesive tape.
12. Two $1/8$-in. (3-mm) sheets of lead.
13. Direct read-out dosimeter.
14. Stopwatch.
15. Low-contrast test pattern with two sets of four holes of the following sizes:
    a. 1.0 mm.
    b. 3.0 mm.
    c. 5.0 mm.
    d. 7.0 mm.
16. Electronic x-ray generator timer with interconnecting cable.

Lab #1

Scatter Radiation

Name _____ **Date** _____

Objective

> To record the intensity of scattered radiation from the fluoroscopic x-ray tube at various distances and locations from the table top utilizing different kVp settings.

Materials

1. Ionization chamber-type survey meter (Cutie-pie, Victoreen Condenser R-meter).
2. Phantom part: chest, abdomen, pelvis, skull, or CT water bottle.
3. Tape measure or ruler.
4. Protective apparel.
5. Personnel monitoring device.

© GR/St. Lucie Press

■ Principles of Fluoroscopic Image Intensification and Television Systems: Workbook and Laboratory Manual

Procedure

1. Center the phantom to the midline of the table.
2. Position the image intensifier over the phantom part. The image intensifier should be placed 6 in. above the phantom part (see Figure A).
3. Using proper protective apparel, position the ionization chamber between the image intensifier and the table top (see Figure A).
4. Select the fluoroscopic technique using 80 kVp and 120 kVp.
5. Turn beam "ON" and record the exposure rate (mR/hr.) at 1-ft, 2-ft, and 3-ft distances and at various locations around the fluoroscopic table.

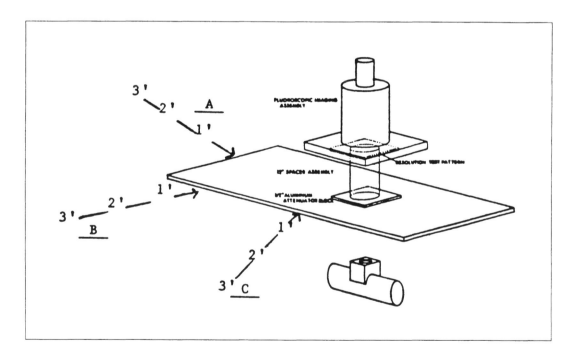

Figure A

Record Data

80 kVp

1 ft	2 ft	3 ft
a. _____ mR/hr.	_____ mR/hr.	_____ mR/hr.
b. _____ mR/hr.	_____ mR/hr.	_____ mR/hr.
c. _____ mR/hr.	_____ mR/hr.	_____ mR/hr.

120 kVp

1 ft	2 ft	3 ft
a. _____ mR/hr.	_____ mR/hr.	_____ mR/hr.
b. _____ mR/hr.	_____ mR/hr.	_____ mR/hr.
c. _____ mR/hr.	_____ mR/hr.	_____ mR/hr.

Analysis

Analyze and compare the recorded data using different kVp levels, distances, and locations from the table top.

Conclusion

1. Summarize the effects of 80 kVp and 120 kVp with regard to intensity, distance, and location on scatter radiation.

■ Principles of Fluoroscopic Image Intensification and Television Systems: Workbook and Laboratory Manual

2. Using the recorded data at the different kVp settings, distances, and locations, calculate the technologist's exposure if there were 5 min. of beam "ON" time.

80 kVp

1 ft	2 ft	3 ft
a. _____ mR	_____ mR	_____ mR
b. _____ mR	_____ mR	_____ mR
c. _____ mR	_____ mR	_____ mR

120 kVp

1 ft	2 ft	3 ft
a. _____ mR	_____ mR	_____ mR
b. _____ mR	_____ mR	_____ mR
c. _____ mR	_____ mR	_____ mR

3. Analyze the recorded data from question #2. What personnel protection techniques should be employed during fluoroscopic examinations?

© GR/St. Lucie Press

Lab #2

Source-to-Table-Top Distance

Name _____ Date _____

Objective

> To evaluate the design and operation of the fluoroscope for compliance with acceptable conditions of radiation control. To determine the minimum distance from the focal spot of the x-ray tube to the surface of the table top.

Materials

1. Image-intensified fluoroscope.
2. Quarter or fifty-cent coin.
3. Tape measure or ruler.
4. Spot-film cassette.
5. Spot-film device.
6. Personnel protective apparel and monitoring device.

© GR/St. Lucie Press

Procedure

1. Position the entrance surface of the fluoroscopic imaging assembly 12 in. above the top surface of the table and lock the vertical travel of the imaging assembly (see Figure A).
2. Place the metal coin on the table top.
3. Under fluoroscopic control, move the fluoroscopic imaging assembly longitudinally and transversely until the coin is in the viewed fluoroscopic image and lock the fluoroscopic assembly in place.
4. Place a spot-film cassette in the spot-film device, Program 1:1.
5. For fluoroscopic equipment with manual control, select 80–100 mAs in the 60–80-kVp range and expose the film for 1–2 min. For fluoroscopic systems that operate only in the automatic brightness control mode, the kVp and the mA will be automatically adjusted.
6. Make a spot-film exposure and process the film.

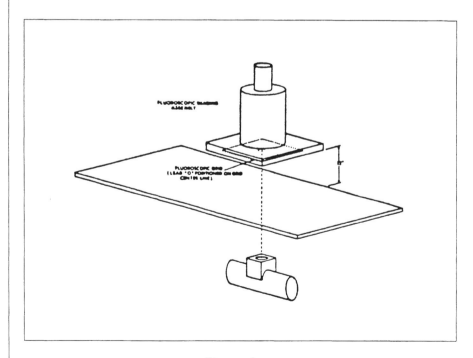

Figure A

Analysis

To carry out the required calculations, it will be necessary to make measurements of certain dimensions on the test film. These measurements should be carefully carried out and made to the nearest 0.03 in.

To calculate the distance of the x-ray tube target to the table top, the following formula is used:

$$STTD = \frac{(TTID)\ O/I}{(1-O/I)}$$

Where:

STTD = Source-to-table-top distance

TTID = Table-top-to-image distance

O = Object size (diameter of the coin)

I = Image size (diameter of the image)

Conclusion

1. Calculate the tube target position.

    (O) Object size = _____ in.

    (I) Image size = _____ in.

    (TTID) Table-top-to-image receptor distance = _____ in.

    (STTD) Source-to-table-top distance = _____ in.

2. Is the measured STTD ≤15 in.? __ Yes __ No

© GR/St. Lucie Press

Lab #3

Grid Alignment

Name _____ Date _____

Objective

> To verify the proper alignment of the grid used in conjunction with image-intensified fluoroscopic equipment.

Materials

1. Image-intensified fluoroscope.
2. Radiopaque "O" marker.
3. Spot-film cassette.
4. Spot-film device.
5. Personnel protective apparel and monitoring device.

Procedure

1. Prepare the system for operation in the fluoroscopic mode.

© GR/St. Lucie Press

2. If the system is equipped with a slide back grid, move the grid to the position it would normally occupy during fluoroscopic imaging (see Figure A).

3. Position the image receptor 12 in. above the table top and lock in place.

4. Observe the direction of the grid lines with respect to the length of the fluoroscopic table (parallel or perpendicular) and record on the following page.

5. Using a piece of tape, affix the lead "O" marker to the face of the grid so that it is centered on the indicated center line of the grid.

6. If the system is equipped with fluoroscopic imaging only, initiate fluoroscopic imaging with the largest intensifier mode and observe the image of the lead "O" on the available viewing means and slowly reduce the size of the radiation field to obtain a small square around the image of the marker. **The marker should be at the center of the field of view**.

7. If the system is equipped with a spot-film device, insert a loaded spot-film cassette into the spot-film device and make a spot-film exposure at low kVp and mA. Process the test film.

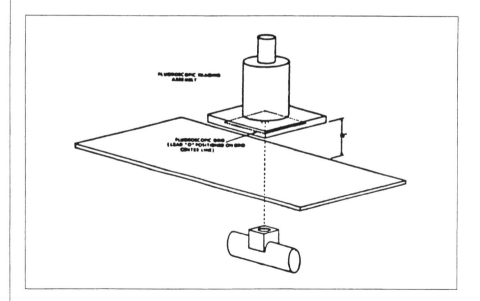

Figure A: Illustration of equipment setup for performing test.

Analysis

1. For systems that do not incorporate spot-film devices, simply observe and record as acceptable or unacceptable the degree of congruence between the radiopaque marker and the viewed image with respect to that direction to which lines of the grid are parallel.

2. For systems with spot-film devices, determine the center line of the process test film perpendicular to the direction of grid lines and measure and record the distance between the "O" marker again only in that direction perpendicular to the grid.

Conclusion

1. Equipment identification   _____

2. Grid ratio   _____

3. Grid frequency (lines/ in. or lines/cm)   _____

4. Target-to-receptor distance   _____

5. Source-to-table-top distance   _____

6. Grid height above table   _____

7. Adequacy of grid alignment   _____ acceptable/unacceptable

8. Remarks/comments

Lab #4

Fluoroscopic Resolution Test

Name _____ Date _____

Objective

> A quality assurance test to determine if the system has suffered a loss in imaging resolving power.

Materials

1. Fluoroscopic resolution test tool.
2. $7\frac{7}{8}$-in. lucite phantom.
3. Under-the-table x-ray tube.
4. Tape.
5. Personnel protective devices.

Procedure

1. Set fluoroscopic machine on automatic brightness mode.
2. Set fluoroscopic control to 50 kVp and 1 mA, if available.

© GR/St. Lucie Press

■ Principles of Fluoroscopic Image Intensification and Television Systems: Workbook and Laboratory Manual

3. Place a $7^{7}/_{8}$-in. lucite phantom on the table top.
4. Tape the resolution test device as close to the image intensifier as possible.
5. Place the fluoroscopic tower 12 in. from the table.
6. View the resolution test tool on the television monitor. Record the results.

Analysis

Maximum resolution will be at the center of the field.

Conclusion

1. A 6-in. image intensifier tube will resolve 30–35 mesh numbers at the center (number of wires/in.).
   Record results _____
2. A 6-in. intensifier tube will resolve 24–30 mesh numbers at the periphery.
   Record results _____

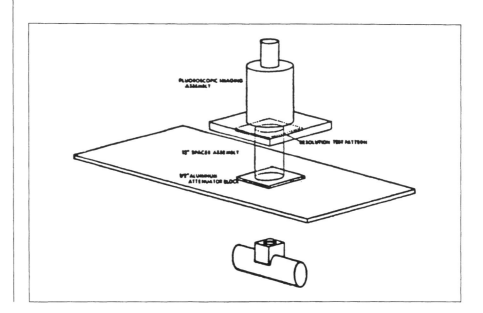

Lab #5

Maximum Fluoroscopic Exposure Rate

Name _____ Date _____

Objective

> To assure an exposure rate adequate to perform quality fluoroscopic examinations on patients of all sizes. To assure that the fluoroscopic unit meets the Bureau of Radiologic Health maximum exposure rates.

Materials

1. Two $1/8$-in. (3-mm) sheets of lead.
2. Direct read-out dosimeter.
3. $7\,7/8$-in. lucite phantom.
4. Stopwatch.
5. Under-the-table x-ray tube.
6. Personnel protective devices.

© GR/St. Lucie Press

Procedure

1. Set the fluoroscopic machine controls on automatic brightness mode.
2. Turn the mA and kVp controls to maximum, if available.
3. Place the dosimeter on table top.
4. Position the dosimeter in the center of the radiation field using the fluoroscope.
5. Adjust the collimators.
6. Turn the dosimeter to exposure rate control.
7. Place a $7\frac{7}{8}$-in. lucite phantom above the ionization chamber.
8. Place the fluoroscopic tower 12 in. from the table top.
9. Place two $\frac{1}{8}$-in. sheets of lead on the lucite phantom above the ion chamber.
10. Fluoroscope long enough for the ABS to stabilize, making sure the beam is attenuated. You should not be able to see light on the television monitor.
11. Read and record the exposure rate. Indicate mA and kVp.
12. Place the fluoroscopic machine in the manual mode with the mA and kVp controls at the maximum settings.
13. Read and record the exposure rate.

Analysis

BRH regulations for equipment certification state that the maximum fluoroscopic exposure rate shall not exceed 5 R/min. in the manual mode and shall not exceed 10 R/min. in the automatic exposure mode.

Conclusion

1. Automatic brightness control mode
   _____ R/min.
   _____ mA
   _____ kVp

2. Manual mode
   _____ R/min.
   _____ mA
   _____ kVp

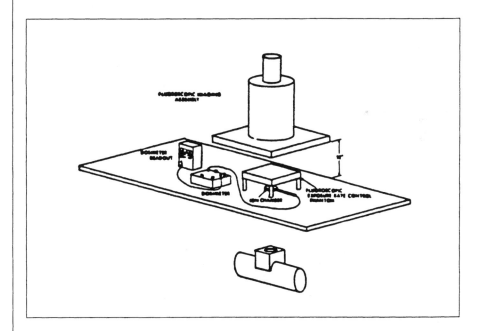

Lab #6

Fluoroscopy Low-Contrast Performance

Name _____ Date _____

Objective

To visually check for the ability of the imaging system to display low-contrast information.

Materials

1. Two $3/4$-in. aluminum plates.
2. One sheet of 1.0-mm Al, with two sets of four holes of the following sizes:
    a. 1.0 mm
    b. 3.0 mm
    c. 5.0 mm
    d. 7.0 mm

© GR/St. Lucie Press

Procedure

1. Place the two aluminum blocks on the table top. The low-contrast pattern should be placed on top of the aluminum plates.
2. Place the image intensifier assembly 12 in. from the table top.
3. Select 80 kVp and adjust the mA to give the best image.
4. Adjust the television monitor while executing fluoroscopy to achieve the best low-contrast performance.

Analysis

1. There are two rows of equally sized and shaped holes. You should see both holes of the same size in order to count them as a "ONE HOLE SET."
2. Record the maximum number of hole sets:

   _____ mm   _____ mm
   _____ mm   _____ mm

3. Record the following:

   Operating kVP _____

   Operating mA _____

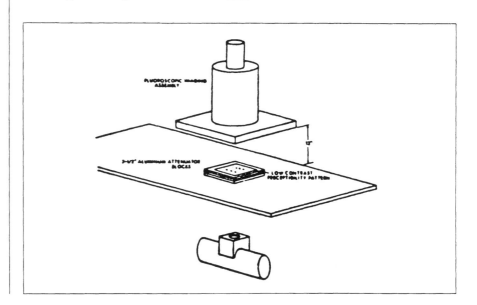

Lab #7

Automatic Exposure Control Evaluation for Film Recording System/Reproducibility

Name _____ Date _____

Objective

> To evaluate the performance of the automatic exposure control system for film recording using the spot-film device.

Materials

1. Two 1-in. aluminum phantometers.
2. Digital x-ray generator timer with remote detector and interconnecting cable.
3. Lead numbers for film identification.
4. Three film/screen cassettes.

© GR/St. Lucie Press

■ Principles of Fluoroscopic Image Intensification and Television Systems: Workbook and Laboratory Manual

5. Ruler.
6. Densitometer.

Procedure

1. Place the aluminum phantom on the table top and under the fluoroscopic control; center the phantom with respect to the viewed fluoroscopic image.

2. Position the beam entrance surface of the fluoroscopic imaging assembly 12 in. above the table top and lock the fluoroscopic tower in place vertically.

3. Adjust the beam restriction system so that it is open to its maximum extent or operation in the automatic mode.

4. Position the remote detector for the x-ray generator timer at the table top under the aluminum phantom.

5. Insert a loaded cassette in the spot-film device.

6. Select 80 kVp on the x-ray generator and the mA system most commonly used for the AEC exposures.

7. Select the normal density control, if such a selection is available.

8. In succession, make three automatically controlled exposures. Change the film cassettes for each exposure.

9. Record the exposure times on the data form. Use the lead numbers to identify each test film.

10. Process the three test films, measure the film density of the phantom, and record the results on the data form.

Laboratory Experiment #7 ▪ Automatic Exposure Control Evaluation

Analysis

Calculate and record the average exposure time and film density obtained. Compare the individual recorded measurements with the average values. A properly functioning automatic exposure control system (phototimer) may be operated to provide reproducibility to within 5% or better.

Conclusion

Reproducibility/Spot Screen Film System

Test Condition: 80 kVp _____ mA

Normal density

2-in. phantom thickness

Test Film #	Measured Exposure Time	Measured Film Density
#1	_____	_____
#2	_____	_____
#3	_____	_____
Average Exposure Time	_____	
Average Film Density	_____	
Maximum Exposure Time Variation	_____	
Maximum Film Density Variation	_____	

© GR/St. Lucie Press

1. Is the automatic exposure control functioning properly for reproducibility? Explain your answer.

2. Would using a number of cassettes for the reproducibility test of the generator produce more or less uniformity of the density data? Explain your answer.

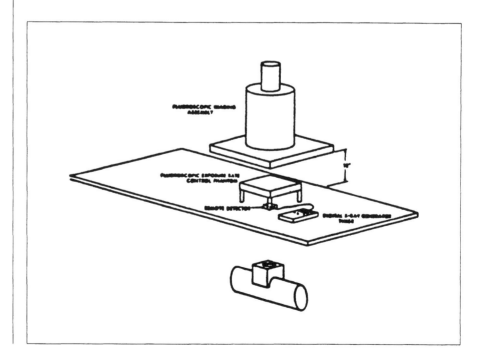

Appendix E

Glossary

Absorbed Dose: The energy imparted by ionizing radiation per unit mass of irradiated material. The units of absorbed dose are the Rad and the Gray (Gy).

ALARA: An acronym for *As Low As Reasonably Achievable*. It is the philosophy for maintaining occupational radiation exposures as low as reasonably achievable. This concept is the basis for the radiation protection goal of reducing doses whenever possible in order to reduce any unnecessary risk.

Ampere: The unit of electrical current equal to the steady current produced by one volt applied across a resistance of one ohm. This electrical current determines the quantity of x-rays produced at the anode of the x-ray tube.

Angular Magnification: A measure of the angle subtended at the eye by an object compared to some fixed standard reference. The object for the eye may be a real or virtual image created in the optical instrument.

Anode: A positive electrode, also referred to as a *target*, to which electrons originating at the cathode are attracted. When these electrons hit the anode or target, some of their kinetic energy is converted to x-rays.

Attenuation: The process by which a beam of radiation is reduced in intensity when passing through material.

Automatic Exposure Control: A device that automatically controls one or more technical factors in order to obtain at a prescribed location(s) a required quantity of radiation.

Bandwidth, Bandpass: The total number of cycles per unit of time (usually one second) that may be used to modulate the electron beam in a television camera.

Barrier, Primary: Barrier sufficient to attenuate the useful beam to the required degree.

Barrier, Protective: Barrier of attenuating materials used to reduce radiation exposure.

Barrier, Secondary: Barrier sufficient to attenuate stray radiation to the required degree.

Beam Splitter: An optical element used to divide a beam of light so that it may

© GR/St. Lucie Press

be simultaneously projected in two different directions.

Bergonie and Tribondeau, Law of: The empirical rule which states that the radiosensitivity of tissues depends on the number of undifferentiated cells which the tissue contains, the degree of mitotic activity in the tissue, and the length of time the cells of the tissue stay in active proliferation.

Boost Position: The high-level control setting of fluoroscopic equipment that enables it to override routine exposure limits.

Cine Camera: A camera used for recording motion—in cinefluoroscopy, one which usually visualizes either 16 or 35mm film. Frame rates may be on the order of 15–60 frames/sec.

Cineradiography or Cine: The making of a motion picture record of successive images appearing on a fluorescent screen.

Collective Dose: The sum of the individual doses received in a given period of time by a specified population from exposure to a specified source of radiation.

Compliance Test: A test which is performed on x-ray equipment to ensure that the x-ray unit meets the radiation safety regulation.

Composite Video Signal: The composite television signal transmitted from the camera consisting of three parts—video, blanking, and synchronizing pulses.

Compression Cone: An attachment for use in fluoroscopy of the GI tract which serves to permit the examiner to apply pressure to various parts being examined, displace some of the overlying structures, and improve the examination.

Contrast (fluoroscopic image): The ratio of the brightness on the open field at a given exposure to the brightness underneath a lead disk covering 10% of the useful central imaging area in a second exposure. Contrast for modern image intensifiers exceeds 15:1.

Conversion Factor: The quotient of the luminescence of the output phosphor of the image intensifier divided by the kerma rate at the input phosphor. The recommended means of expressing the luminance gain of an image intensifier tube. Defined as being the ratio of the output screen luminance in candela per square meter to the input exposure rate in millirads per second.

Creep: The horizontal or vertical movement of fluoroscopic equipment during an x-ray examination.

Dead-Man Switch: A switch so constructed that a circuit closing contact may only be maintained with continuous pressure by the operator.

Diagnostic-Type Tube Housing: X-ray tube housing so constructed that the leakage radiation at a distance of one meter from the target cannot exceed 100 milliRoentgen in one hour when the x-ray tube is operated at any of its specified ratings.

Diffraction: The spreading of a beam of light or other electromagnetic radiation when passing through an aperture or over an opaque edge.

Digital Radiography: A diagnostic procedure using an appropriate radiation source and an imaging system that collects, processes, stores, recalls, and presents image formation in a digital rather than analog fashion.

Digital Subtraction: An image processing procedure used to improve image contrast by subtracting one digital image from another.

Digital-to-Analog Converter (DAC): A device that converts digital signals into analog signals.

Direct Effect: The effect of ionizing particles interacting directly with (transferring their energy to) biologic macromolecules such as DNA, RNA, ATP, proteins, or enzymes. The chemical bonds of these macromolecules break, and they become abnormal structures.

Distortion: Unequal magnification of different portions of the body area being x-rayed. A variation in magnification across the field of an image. If a camera lens has distortion, the image it produces (of a square object) will have curved lines leading to either barrel or pincushion shapes.

Dose: A general term denoting the quantity of radiation or energy absorbed per unit mass. For special purposes, it must be appropriately qualified. If qualified, it refers to absorbed dose.

> **Absorbed Dose**: The energy imparted to matter by ionizing radiation per unit mass of irradiated material at a place of interest. The unit of absorbed dose is the Rad.

One Rad equals 100 ergs per gram. The SI unit for absorbed dose is the Gray (Gy): 1 Gy = 1 joule/kg.

Dose Equivalent: A quantity used in radiation protection. It expresses all radiations on a common scale for calculating the effective absorbed dose. It is defined as the product of the absorbed dose in Rads and the Quality Factor of the radiation. The unit of dose equivalent is the Rem. In the SI system, the special unit of dose equivalent is the Sievert (Si): 1 Si = 1 joule/kg.

Gonad Dose: The amount of radiation absorbed by the gonads resulting from any part of the body being exposed to x-rays.

Dosimeter: An instrument used to detect and measure accumulated radiation exposure.

Duty Factor: The ratio of on-to-off time of some machine or process. A 100% duty factor would indicate continual usage. A 50% duty factor would indicate an average of half off and half on.

Dynamic Radiography: Radiographic procedures that allow the visualization of motion.

Effective Dose Equivalent (H_E): The sum of the products of the dose equivalent to the organ or tissue (H_T) and the weighting factor (W_T) applicable to each of the body organs or tissues that are irradiated.

Electromagnetic Radiation: A traveling wave motion resulting from changing electric or magnetic fields. Familiar electromagnetic radiations range from x-ray or short wavelength, through ultraviolet, visible, and infrared regions, to radar and radiowaves of relatively long wavelength.

Electron Volt: A unit of energy equivalent to the energy gained by an electron in passing through a potential difference of one volt. Large multiple units of electron volts are frequently used—KeV for thousand or kiloelectron volts, MeV for million or mega electron volts.

Erg: The amount of work done by a force of one dyne acting through a distance of one centimeter. Unit of energy which can exert a force of one dyne through a distance of one centimeter. It is equal to 10^{-7} joules (unit of work).

Exposure: The amount of ionization produced in air by x- or gamma radiation. It is the sum of the electrical charges on all ions of one sign produced in air when all electrons liberated by photons in a volume element of air are completely stopped in air, divided by the mass of the air in the volume element. The special unit of exposure is the roentgen: $1 R = 2.58 \times 10^{-4}$.

    Acute Exposure: Radiation exposure of short duration.

    Chronic Exposure: Radiation exposure over a long duration by fractionation or protraction.

Eye Dose Equivalent: Applies to the external exposure of the lens of the eye and is taken as the dose equivalent at a tissue depth of 0.3 cm (300 mg/cm).

f/number: The term used to denote the relative speed of a camera lens. The f/number of a lens is equal to its focal length divided by its diameter.

Film Badge: A personnel monitoring device. The film badge device records radiation exposure accumulated at a low rate over a long period of time (usually one month). An assembly containing a packet of unexposed photographic film and a variety of filters (absorbers).

Filter: Material placed in the useful beam to absorb preferentially the less penetrating radiation.

    Added Filtration: Sheets of metal (usually aluminum or its equivalent) that are placed in the direct path of the x-ray beam.

    Inherent Filtration: The x-ray tube and its housing, such as the glass envelope through which the x-ray beam passes.

Fluoroscopy: A radiological examination using fluorescence for observation of the transient image.

Flux Gain: Increase in output image brightness from an image intensifier tube expressed as a ratio of the number of light photons at the output screen to the number of light photons produced at the input screen.

Focal Length: A property of all lenses. That distance from the lens at which the lens will image an infinitely distant object.

Format: The film frame size of a photographic camera. The scanning area of a pick-up tube in a television camera.

Frame Rate: In cine or television cameras, that number of sequential pictures per unit of time (usually one second) that are displayed.

Framing Frequency: The number of frames of film per second (f/s).

Gram: A metric unit of mass and weight nearly equal to 1 cm^3 of water at its maximum density.

Half Value Layer: The thickness of a specified substance which, when introduced into the path of a given beam of radiation, reduces the exposure rate by one half.

Health Physics: The science of protecting human beings from injury by radiation and of promoting better health through beneficial applications of radiation.

High Radiation Area: Any area, accessible to individuals, in which radiation levels could result in an individual receiving a dose equivalent in excess of 0.1 Rem (1 mSv) in 1 hour at 30 cm from the radiation source or from any surface that the radiation penetrates.

Horizontal Retrace: That period of time during which the electron beam is repositioned following the completion of one horizontal line in preparation for starting the next horizontal line.

ICRP: The International Commission on Radiological Protection, established in 1928 by the Second International Congress of Radiology. It prepares recommendations to deal with the basic principles of radiation protection.

Image Intensifier: A device used to convert an x-ray image into a light image, then to an electron image, and then back to a light image of smaller size and increased brightness.

Image Receptor: A system for deriving a diagnostically usable image from the x-rays transmitted by the patient. Examples are screen film systems, stimulatable phosphor, and solid state detectors.

Indirect Effect: Destructive chemical changes in body molecules that result when a specific molecule such as DNA is acted upon by free radicals which were previously produced from the interaction of radiation with water molecules.

Integral Dose: A calculated dose for a portion of the body determined by the size of the field, the skin dose, and the depth of tissue at which the dose falls to one half the skin dose.

Interlace: The method by which sequential television fields are displayed on the kinescope. The two types are positive interlace and random interlace.

Inverse Square Law: The intensity of the radiation is inversely proportional to the square of the distance from the source.

Kell Factor A factor used to correct idealized vertical resolving power to that which would be realized in actual usage. Generally taken to have a value of 0.7.

Kerma: The sum of the initial kinetic energies of all the charged ionizing particles liberated by uncharged ionizing particles per unit mass of a specified material. Measured in the same unit as absorbed dose. The SI unit of kerma is joule per kilogram, and its special name is Gray (Gy). Kerma can be quoted for any specified material at a point in free space or in an absorbing medium.

Kinescope: The display or picture tube of the monitor.

Lag: The undesirable quality of most vidicon (television) tubes that occurs because it takes a certain amount of time for the image to build up and decay on the vidicon target. This results in image blurring when the camera is moved rapidly during fluoroscopy.

Linear Hypothesis: The assumption that a dose effect curve derived from data in the high dose rate ranges may be extrapolated through the low dose range to zero. This implies that any amount of radiation can cause some damage.

Linearity: The ability of a television system to faithfully reproduce an object with the correct dimensions and proportions. Pool linearity will cause a non-uniform elongation or foreshortening of the image.

Magnetic Recording: A means of obtaining a permanent record of an electrical signal. Converts the signal to a magnetic field, which is used to permanently magnetize some storage medium. Common devices are video tape recorders and video disc recorders.

Magnification: The ratio of image size to object size. The image may be larger than, smaller than, or equal to the object; so magnification can be greater than, equal to, or less than 1.

Magnification Mode: Occurs when the useful area of the input phosphor is decreased (6-in. mode) while the output phosphor remains the same size, thus increasing the effective magnification of the resultant image. Concurrently, the collimator automatically reduces the x-ray field to the usable input phosphor area.

Maximum Permissible Dose: The greatest dose equivalent that a person or specified part thereof shall be allowed to receive in a given period of time.

Milliampere (mA): A measure of x-ray tube current of which the intensity of an x-ray beam is a function; mA multiplied by the time during which the beam strikes an object is milliampere-seconds and is a measure of the quantity of x-ray.

Minification Gain: The increase in output image brightness from an image intensifier tube that results from reduction in image size; expressed as the ratio of $(d_i/d_o)^2$.

Mobile Intensifier: An integrated system of x-ray generator, x-ray tube, and image intensifier. A self-contained unit that may be moved to different locations.

Modulation Transfer Function (MTF): A mathematical entity that expresses the relative responses of an imaging system or system component to sinusoidal inputs as a function of varying spatial frequency, which is often expressed in line pairs per millimeter (lp/mm). The MTF can be thought of as a measure of spatial resolution of the detector system.

Mutation: A transformation of the gene that may be induced by radiation and may alter characteristics of the offspring.

NCRP: The National Council on Radiation Protection and Measurements, a non-profit corporation chartered by Congress in 1964. The concern of NCRP is with the scientific and technical aspects of radiation protection.

Non-stochastic Effect: Health effects of radiation in which the severity varies with the dose and for which a threshold is believed to exist. Radiation-induced cataract formation is an example of a non-stochastic effect. This is also called a *deterministic effect*.

Objective Lens: The lens that collects the light from the output screen and projects it into the camera lens or into the optical viewer.

Operator's Station: The area where the control panel for the operator of an x-ray machine is located.

Out-of-Phase: Opposite of in-phase. The periodic motions do not occur in each compartment at the same time; $180°$ out-of-phase means that at any given time they are exactly opposite.

Pan and Tilt Controls: Motorized motions of the television camera. The camera may be aimed at different directions to change the field of view.

Panel: The table top of the imaging unit as a whole.

Personnel Monitoring Equipment: Devices designed to be worn or carried by an individual for the purpose of measuring the dose received by that individual (e.g., film badges, pocket dosimeters, film rings, thermoluminescent dosimeters, etc.).

Photocathode: A material rich in electrons, which can be made to emit electrons under the action of incident light.

Photoelectric Absorption: An interaction between an x-ray photon and an orbital electron in which the photon surrenders all of its kinetic energy to the electron and ceases to exist. The atom responds by ejecting the electron from the shell. Photoelectric absorption is the process most responsible for the dose of radiation the patient receives during a radiographic procedure.

Photomultiplier: A type of vacuum tube used to achieve electron gains. For example, one incident electron will create two secondary electrons that may, in turn, be used to create four secondary electrons.

Positive Interlace: One type of interlace pattern in which two or more fields are precisely positioned among each other. The most common positive interlace is a two-to-one type, wherein two television fields are used to create one television frame.

Primary Barrier: A barrier sufficient to attenuate the useful beam to the required degree.

Quality Assurance (QA): A management tool that includes policies and procedures designed to optimize the performance of facility personnel and equipment. QA includes (1) quality control, (2) administration, (3) education of personnel, and (4) preventive maintenance methods.

Quality Control (QC): Refers to routine performance and interpretation of test equipment function and to corrective action needed and taken.

Quantum Mottle/Noise: Statistical fluctuations in the radiographic image that results in a grainy appearance. Mottle is more visible in a high-resolution, high-contrast image.

Quantum Sink: The variation in optical density, brightness, CT number, or other appropriate parameter in an image that results from the random spatial distribution of the x-ray or light quanta absorbed at the state of the imaging chain containing the minimum information content. The quantum sink of a correctly tuned fluoroscopy imaging system with closed circuit television camera is the number of x-ray photons absorbed by the image intensifier input phosphor.

Radiation: Gamma rays and x-rays, alpha and beta particles, high-speed electrons, neutrons, protons, and other nuclear particles—not sound or radio waves, or visible, infrared, or ultraviolet light.

Radiation Safety Officer: The person responsible for the radiation protection program at a medical facility.

Raster: The scanning pattern developed in the television kinescope. In most cases, the scan pattern is from upper left to lower right as a series of horizontal lines.

Real Image: An image created by the actual intersection of light rays and defined as being one which can be displayed on a diffusing screen.

Refraction: The bending of a beam of energy that passes across an interface of material with different indices or refraction.

Relative Aperture: A measure of the light-gathering ability of a lens. Expressed mathematically as the ratio of the focal length divided by the diameter of the lens entrance pupil. The number determined by this calculation is frequently referred to as the f/number.

Rem: The special unit of any of the quantities expressed as dose equivalent. The dose equivalent in Rems is equal to the absorbed dose in Rads multiplied by the quality factor.

Resolution: The process or capability of distinguishing closely adjacent optical images.

Retrace: That part of the scanning system during which the electron beam is returned to a starting point after completing a line or field.

Secondary or Stray Radiation: Radiation not serving any useful purpose. It includes leakage and scattered radiation.

Shallow Dose Equivalent (H_s): Applies to the external exposure of the skin and an extremity and is taken as the dose equivalent at a tissue depth of 0.007 cm (7 mg/cm^2) averaged over an area of 1 cm^2.

Shield/Shielding: Material which is interposed between a radiation source and an irradiated site for the purpose of minimizing the radiation hazard. Shielding is usually made of lead, which is dense and absorbs radiation easily. Shielding is often used to protect the reproductive organs from the x-ray beam during an examination.

Sievert: The SI unit of any of the quantities expressed as dose equivalent. The dose equivalent in Sieverts is equal to the absorbed dose in Grays multiplied by the quality factor of the radiation.

Simulator: Diagnostic energy x-ray equipment used to simulate a therapy treatment plan outside the treatment room.

Source-Surface Distance (Source-Skin Distance) (SSD): The distance measured along the central ray from the center of the front surface of the source (x-ray focal spot) to the surface of the irradiated object or patient.

Spot Film: An image taken to document the patient's anatomy at specific moments during fluoroscopy. Spot films may be obtained by using a radiographic cassette or by photographing the output of the image intensifier with a spot-film camera.

Stochastic Effect: Health effects that occur randomly and for which the probability of the effect occurring, rather than its severity, is assumed to be a linear function of dose without threshold. Hereditary effects and cancer incidence are examples of stochastic effects.

Synchronization: The operation of the camera shutters at the same frequency as the x-ray pulse.

Tenth Value Layer: Thickness of a specified substance which, when introduced into the path of a given beam of radiation, reduces the kerma rate to one-tenth of its original rate.

Total Brightness Gain: Minification gain multiplied by the flux gain.

Useful Beam: Means that part of the radiation which passes through the window, aperture, cone, or other collimating device of the tube housing.

Vertical Retrace: That period of time during which the electron beam is blanked and repositioned, after the completion of one television field, to the starting point for the next television field.

Very High Radiation Area: An area, accessible to individuals, in which radiation levels could result in an individual receiving an absorbed dose in excess of 500 Rads (5 Grays) in 1 hour at 1 meter from a radiation source or from any surface that the radiation penetrates.

Vignetting: A decrease in light intensity at the periphery of an image.

Visual Acuity: The ability of the eye to resolve the angular separation of two objects. For the human eye, it is usually between one and two minutes of arc.

Weighting Factor: For an organ or tissue (T), it is the proportion of the risk of stochastic effects resulting from irradiation of that organ or tissue to the total risk of stochastic effects when the whole body is irradiated uniformly.

For calculating the effective dose equivalent, the values of W are:

<u>Organ Dose Weighting Factors</u>	W_T
Gonads	0.25
Breast	0.15
Red Bone Marrow	0.12
Lung	0.12
Thyroid	0.03
Bony surfaces	0.03
Remainder	0.30[1]
Whole body	1.00[2]

(1) 0.30 results from 0.06 for each of the five "remainder" organs, excluding the skin and the lens of the eye, that receive the highest doses.

(2) For the purpose of weighting the external body dose, a single weighting factor has been specified.

Appendix F

Bibliography

Ballinger, P.W. (1986). *Merrill's atlas of radiographic positions and radiologic procedures* (6th ed., Vols. I–III). St. Louis: C.V. Mosby Co.

Barnes, G., & Tishler, J. (1981). Image quality and its implications regarding equipment and selection and use. In Coulam, Erickson, Rollo, and James, Jr. (Eds.), *The physical basis of medical imaging* (pp. 90–106). New York: Appleton-Century-Crofts.

Bontrager, K. (1993). *Textbook of radiographic positioning and related anatomy* (3rd ed.). St. Louis: Mosby Year Book.

Bushong, S. (1995). *Radiologic science for the technologist: Physics, biology, and protection* (5th ed.). St. Louis: C.V. Mosby Co.

———. *Radiologic science: Workbook and laboratory manual* (5th ed.). St. Louis: C.V. Mosby Co.

California Department of Health Services, Radiologic Health Branch. (1995). *Syllabus on fluoroscopic radiation protection.* Sacramento, CA.

Coulam, C., Erickson, J., Rollo, F., & James, A. (1981). *The physical basis of medical imaging.* New York: Appleton-Century-Crofts.

Curry, T., Dowdey, J., & Murry, R. (1984). *Christensen's introduction to the physics of diagnostic radiology* (3rd ed.). Philadelphia: Lea and Febiger.

Gray, J., Winkler, M., Stears, J., & Frank, E. (1983). *Quality control in diagnostic imaging.* Rockville, MD: Aspen Publishers.

Hendee, W., & Rossi, R. *Quality assurance for fluoroscopic x-ray units and associated equipment.* HEW Publication, FDA 80-8095.

Mallett, M. (1981). *Handbook of anatomy and physiology for students of medical radiation technology* (3rd ed.). Mankato, MN: The Burnell Co., Inc.

© GR/St. Lucie Press

Rich, J. (1969). *The theory and application of intensified fluoroscopy in the radiology department.* Milwaukee: General Electric Co.

————. *The theory and application of television in the radiology department.* Milwaukee: General Electric Co.

Sidband, M. (1981). Fluoroscopic imaging. In Coulam, Erickson, Rollo, and James, Jr. (Eds.), *The physical basis of medical imaging* (pp. 75–92). New York: Appleton-Century-Crofts.

Index

A

ABS stabilization circuits 16
Accelerating anode 4
Acceptance testing 166
ALARA 105, 168
Allowable x-ray beam 88
Amplitude 75
Anode 32
Apron/glove integrity 174
Audible signal 90
Automatic brightness
    control 170
    stabilization 13, 88
Automatic exposure control 88, 123
    evaluation 217

B

Bandwidth 36
Bone marrow 94
Boost
    fluoroscopy 90
    position 88, 129
Bremsstrahlung radiation 77
Brightness 42
    gain 7, 9
    sensing 15
    stabilizers 16

C

C-arm 127–129
California Radiation Control Regulations
    134, 137, 144
Camera
    control unit 37
    pick-up tubes 30
    tube construction 31
Carcinogenic effects 101

Cataractogenic effects 103
Cellular damage 97
Cessation of cell division 98
Characteristic radiation 78
Charge-coupled device 44
Cine camera 53
Cinefluororadiography 53, 70
Collimation 86
Compliance 201
Compression device 169
Compton scattering 80, 81
Computerized fluoroscopy 65
Contrast 12, 42, 59
Conversion factor and gain 7, 8
Cumulative manual reset timer 88
Cumulative occupational dose equivalent
    118

D

Deflecting coils 32
Department of Health Services 135
Dermatology Supervisor 133
Differential absorption 86
Digital techniques 68
Display contrast 59
Display of documents 134
Distance 140
Distortion 12, 174
Dose effect curves 99
Dose equivalent limits 117
Double contrast knee arthrogram 156
Dual field image intensifier tubes 5

E

Electromagnetic focusing coils 32
Electromagnetic radiation 73
Electron gun 31
Electrostatic focusing lens 4

© GR/St. Lucie Press

Embryological effects 102
Equipment provisions 128
Exact framing 55
Exposure
    rates 88
    recording 117
    reduction 107
    reproducibility 175
    time 87

F

f/number 55
Field 35
Field of view 24
Film badge 115
Film/screen spot-film device 58
Filtration 87
Filtration (HVL measurement) test 172
Five-minute timer test 172
Flat contact shield 146
Fluoroscopic
    beam size test 172
    resolution test 209
    resolution test tool 196
    spot films 155
    tower 169
Fluoroscopy Supervisor 132, 138
Flux gain 8
Focal length 22
Focusing cell 32
Framing 54, 55
Frequency 75

G

Gain control system test 171
Gallbladder fluoroscopy 155
Genetic dose indicators 94
Genetic effects 103
Genetically significant dose 95
Gonadal shielding 123, 146
Grid alignment 205
Gross cellular effects of radiation 98
Guidelines 147

H

Half value layer (HVL) 150
High-contrast resolution test 171

High-level control 88, 129
Horizontal resolution 41
Horizontal scan lines 30

I

Image
    intensifier photocathode current 15
    intensifier tube 2
    lag 174
    quality 10
Image-orthicon cameras 43
Imaging resolving power 209
Incident Notification Requirements 135
Input phosphor 2
Integration time 149
Intensification gain 7
Interlaced horizontal scanning 35
Inverse square law 131, 140
Ionization chamber-type survey meter 195
Isoexposure profile 107

K

K-edge image intensification 68
Kell factor 44
Kiloelectron volt 76
Kilovoltage 169
    accuracy 173
    peak 86
Knee arthrography 156

L

Lag 43
Latent period 98
Lateral meniscus 157
Law of Bergonie and Tribondeau 100
Leakage radiation 106
Lens-coupled photo tube sensing 15
Licentiates 132
Limited permit x-ray technicians 133, 134
Line pair 11
Localization techniques 153
Location of personnel monitoring device 118
Logarithmic processing 66
Long-term effects 101

Low-absorption table top 89
Low contrast
    performance 215
    performance test 169
    resolution test 172

M

Magnetic recorders 48
Magnetic tape 49
MaS linearity 175
Mask mode image intensification 66
Maximum exposure rates 174, 211
Maximum permissible dose (MPD) 116
Mean annual genetically significant dose 95
Medial meniscus 157
Milliamperage 86, 169
Minification gain 9
Minimum source-to-table-top distance 173
Mobile fluoroscope quality control 129
Mobile image intensification equipment 127
Motion 122

N

National Council on Radiation Protection and Measurements 143
Noise 60
Non-threshold hypothesis 99
Normal viewing distance 149

O

Occupational dose equivalent limits 117
Occupationally exposed women 144
Operator exposure 106
Optics 21
Output phosphor 5
Overexposure of a personnel monitoring device 118
Overframing 56

P

Parallax method 154
Parental protection 123
Patient exposure 55, 87

Pediatric fluoroscopy 121
Penetrometer 171
Personnel monitoring devices 113
Photocathode 2, 4
Photocopic vision 148
Photoelectric effect 80
Photon 75
Phototimers 175
Pincushion distortion 13
Plumbicon camera 43
Pocket ionization chambers 116
Production of Bremsstrahlung radiation 77
Production of x-radiation 76
Protective devices 107, 110

Q

Quality assurance 57, 159–161, 163, 209
    manual 165
Quality control 129, 163
Quantum 75
    mottle 10
    noise 10

R

Radiation control 201
    Regulations 114, 117
Radiography supervisor 132
Radiologic Health Sciences Education Project 143
    technology personnel 137
Radiopaque method 154
Radiosensitivity
    of the cell 100
    of tissues 100
Real images 25
Record keeping requirements 135
Recording head 49
Records for QA test equipment 165
Reduction in dose 140
Refraction 22
Relative aperture 23
Required training 136
Resolution 11, 174
Restrictions 133
Right-angle method 154
Room lighting 149

© GR/St. Lucie Press

S

Safety provisions 137
Scatter 82
    radiation 197
Scintillation 10
Scotopic vision 148
Shadow shield 146
Shaped contact shield 146
Sharpness 60
Shielding 141
Shields 110
Short-term effects 101
Shutters test 170
Single contrast knee arthrogram 156
Skin 94
Somatic dose indicators 93
Source-to-image distance 169
Source-to-table-top distance 201
Spatial resolution 70
Spot film
    camera system 57
    device 58
    film camera exposures 175
    image quality 59
Statement of Competency 181
Structural shielding 127
Students 133
Subject contrast 59
Supervision of radiologic technology
    personnel 137
Supervisors 164
Synchronization 38, 54

T

Table-top dose rate 90
Target-to-panel distance 89
Technologists' fluoroscopy clinical
    instruction 139
Television
    frame 35
    image quality 41
    monitor 39
    scanning system 35

Television camera signal sensing 15
10- and 14-day rule 142
Terminal ileum fluoroscopy 155
Therapeutic abortions 143
Thermionic emission 76
Thermoluminescent dosimeter (TLD)
    115
Thyroid 94
Time 140
    interval difference (TID) mode 67
Total filtration 87
Total overframing 56
Tube current 76, 86
Typical patient exposure rates 173

U

Underframing 55
Unmixed digital techniques 68

V

Variations with x-ray factors 14
Veiling glare 13
Velocity 75
Vertical resolution 41
Victoreen condensor R-meter 195
Video
    disc recorders 51
    signal 33
        frequencies 37
    tape recorders 51
Vignetting 12
Virtual images 25
Visual acuity 149
Visual physiology 148

W

Wavelength 75
Women of child-bearing years 142

X

X-ray equipment safety provisions 137
X-ray interaction with matter 79